TIME POOR
SOUL RICH

60 SECOND SOLUTIONS
& other lengthier remedies for BUSY PROFESSIONAL WOMEN

Anne Winckel

Ark House Press
PO Box 1722, Port Orchard, WA 98366 USA
PO Box 1321, Mona Vale NSW 1660 Australia
PO Box 318 334, West Harbour, Auckland 0661 New Zealand
arkhousepress.com

Cataloguing in Publication Data:
Title: Time Poor Soul Rich
ISBN: 9780994194107 (pbk.)
Subjects: Business / Women
Other Authors/Contributors: Winckel, Anne

Printed and bound in Australia
Design and layout by initiatemedia.net

TIME POOR SOUL RICH

"There is nothing quite like this book, offering hope and wisdom to busy working women. Whether it is the heart-touching stories, soul-enriching tips, encouraging quotes or even the photos showing women through the centuries – there is so much to appreciate and gain from *Time Poor Soul Rich*."
Kara Martin, Associate Dean, Marketplace Institute, Ridley College.

"I am often distracted by the feeling of being committed to everything but doing nothing well. Anne has provided a rich resource to replenish, nurture and integrate our 'self' with the amazing capacity we, professional women, deploy every day."
Claire Rogers, Senior Banking Executive and Director.

"For the first time, I have found a fabulous new book which captures in an easy-to-read format two of the greatest passions in my life – the development of women as leaders plus answers to the topic of how do we nourish our souls? Every woman who is a worker, every family who support and encourage the woman leaders in their midst and every employer of women and men will find this more like a road map for life than a book. Anne Winckel's *Time Poor Soul Rich* provides readers with practical ways to navigate through the challenges of modern living. I recommend you get the book so you can unlock a powerhouse of wisdom into your life."
Wendy Simpson OAM, Chairman Wengeo Group Pty Ltd,
Australian Businesswomen's Hall of Fame Inductee.

"Anne has written a deeply engaging and personal book that is warm, optimistic and full of whimsy and humour. Any busy professional (men too!) will almost certainly recognise themselves in the real-life stories recounted by Anne. A dose of TPSR is uplifting; you will put the book down with a smile on your face, ready to face the world."
Fiona Patrick, Company Director and Management Consultant.

To all of the amazing women who continue to share their stories with me and who juggle so many obligations with so much grace and peace.

Contents

PART B ❧ **Overcoming Obstacles to Soul Enrichment**

Chapter 1

ॐ

Slow Trains and Stopwatches

WHEN I WAS 29 I NEARLY married a psychiatrist. We were actually engaged for almost 12 hours before he suggested I might be better off if I didn't accept his proposal! A couple of months later he promptly married an ex-girlfriend. I suppose I should have been heartbroken and taken offence at being jilted so abruptly, but strangely I was relieved.

Instead of moving to London to be a psychiatrist's wife, I had a whole year free ahead of me. I had taken 12 months of leave without pay from my job.

Slow Trains Through India – What this book is *not* about

My "gap year" turned out to be one of the best years of my life. There were volcanoes in the Philippines, cows with bells in the Swiss Alps, Norwegian fjords, Danish castles, Parisian art galleries, Roman ruins, Greek islands, Scottish lochs, *Les Misérables* in Edinburgh, philosophical retreats in the English countryside, ancient murals by abandoned Albanian playing fields and slow trains through India.

In a nutshell, travelling the world was definitely a very soul enriching experience. It was easy to stay refreshed and inspired when I got a good night's sleep, began my morning in thanks to God and spent my days appreciating the beauty of the world and the amazing breadth of humankind's achievements.

But that's not what this book is about. If soul enrichment were only generated through wonderful personal experiences on a gap year, that would certainly be a short-lived and privileged solution.

This book is also not about time management. If you are looking for guidance about juggling your competing priorities, there are plenty of other resources to go to for help. And finally, this book is not about providing a cure for clinical depression. I am not a psychologist. I am just a time-poor professional woman who has struggled to maintain a rich soul instead of allowing internal numbness to take hold.

Stretched to the Tip of Your Stopwatch – What this book *is* about

Time-poor women can be very focussed at work, exceeding expectations, and very intentional at home, keeping their families in good shape, but they can still leave their own well-being to chance. The message of this book is simple: you can be simultaneously "poor in time" and "rich in soul". These things are not mutually exclusive.

One of the core sources of my personal soul enrichment is being creative with ideas and stories. However, for a long time I felt as if the creativity I had as a child had somehow drained away down some bottomless pit of busyness (or down the "corporate black hole" as I like to call it). Creativity is one of the 16 casualties of a busy life that I explore in the following pages.

As a child I had an over-active imagination. I used to run around our farm (or ride my horse), living out one adventure after another. I composed poems almost from the time I could write, and later short stories. At the age of 16 I was at university, spending six years overloading to complete various degrees. I then taught four different Year 12 subjects in my first four years as a high school teacher. By the time I was 29, I was exhausted and brain-dead. That is one reason I needed that sabbatical year.

Far from writing poems or anything else meaningful, by my late 20s I had got to the point where I could not even read for pleasure. My plight became pretty obvious one day when a colleague brought me a copy of her literature thesis to review. After opening the front cover and starting to read the introduction, I immediately closed the manuscript and handed it back to her. It was a shock to find that I could not even begin to read her work. I was definitely burnt out.

Neglecting the health of my soul meant I ended up feeling more like a shadow than my true self. I was performing well in my job as a teacher, but my soul had imperceptibly drifted into "survival mode".

This book contains a collection of stories from various time-poor women who have battled to maintain the richness of their souls. Many of their ideas and strategies have also kept me sane and whole in the years that followed my brain-dead predicament. Despite the further exhaustion of completing a Master's thesis whilst lecturing full-time, and a subsequent move into legal recruitment followed by the challenge of launching my own business, I have never drifted back to that state where my brain could not cope with anything outside of work. I certainly have a tendency towards being a workaholic, but many of the strategies in this book have provided me with soul food and helped me to keep a check on my soul destroying habits.

There are plenty of work scenarios or seasons in our lives that mean we cannot escape being time-poor. Perhaps you work full-time and also care for sick parents or small children (or small parents and sick children, as one of my witty friends likes to say!). You might be a mergers and acquisitions lawyer who is closing a deal worth millions. What if your volunteer work and community service leave you no time for home duties, let alone paid work? Do you have to submit a tender by a deadline, or perhaps have a dying patient to treat? What if your job is lurching from one never-ending crisis to the next, leaving no spare time to smell the carefully positioned flowers on your office reception counter? What if you are so stretched to the limit that the idea of discretionary time is just a dream, and you don't remember the last time you wiggled your toes in some soft green grass?

Then don't stop reading! This book is written for someone just like you. I believe you can still maintain a rich soul in the context of an incorrigibly busy life. Although this book is written primarily with business and professional women in mind, those who do not identify with that description may also find some wisdom in these pages. The most exhausting and time-poor years for one of my friends were the years when her three children were under five. She describes these years as "just a blur!"

For anyone who feels time-poor, I hope the following chapters will refresh your soul and calm your spirit, even if you are consumed by the demands of a relentless employer or business, or perhaps by responsibilities in the home. I am hoping you will still want to smile and still feel whole and not hollow. That you can feel a sense of hope and not desperation; peace and not despair. That you will know what it is to be a "human being" and not just a "human doing".

So when you are stretched to the tip of your stopwatch, and you are struggling to find even 15 minutes of discretionary time, how do you stop your inner self from lapsing into numbness? That is what this book is about – having a rich soul when you are inescapably time-poor.

Time-Poor Audit – Does this sound like you?

You will probably identify with the "time-poor" label if a few of the following descriptions apply to you:

- You don't eat lunch until 3.00pm on more than one day per week.
- You don't exercise regularly despite multiple New Year's resolutions.
- You don't read for pleasure.
- You don't invite friends to dinner because you are rarely home at dinner time.
- You don't attend to your garden, your knitting, your painting, your writing, your mountain climbing or whatever your passion is.
- You don't see your children perform in their school plays or at their sports events.

- You don't go to the toilet as soon as you need to but hang on longer than is humanly reasonable.
- You don't send cards or greetings to your family and friends in time for their birthdays.
- You don't read the jokes that your friends email to you, instead just hitting the delete button.
- You don't go to the doctor when you need to, and you don't even google your symptoms.
- You don't walk your dog, play with your cat or teach your bird to talk.
- Or you have completely dispensed with all pets, and potentially your partner as well.

Being "time-poor" means having little if any discretionary time – in other words, not being able to use your time in any crazy way you like. This includes not having the freedom to relax, or sleep, or snooze in the sun. Where do you fit on this time-poor spectrum?

How "time-poor" are you?

Very time-poor	1	Zero or almost no spare time at all
	2	Minimal spare time
	3	Satisfactory amounts of spare time
	4	A good amount of spare time
Not time-poor at all	5	Lots of spare time

If you found this question difficult to answer, you could try the "Time Audit Survey" in the Appendix. If you suspect you should have *more* time, you may want to look into time management techniques. But this book is for exactly the person who has minimal spare time for reasons that can't be easily remedied. Equally, this book might help if you are still getting your time management under control, or if your time management training has taught you strategies that have inadvertently side-stepped or sabotaged the care of your soul.

Many of us have learned about prioritising work, avoiding distractions, focussing on goals, overcoming procrastination, managing interruptions, streamlining tasks and saying no to things which threaten our undivided engagement with work. The price we pay for this excellent time management training can sometimes be the soul enrichment we then neglect. We have been too well trained in how to avoid distractions. The following chapters provide ideas on how to re-engage with many neglected aspects of life that are soul enriching.

Soul-Rich Audit – Do you see yourself in this?

You probably won't identify with being rich in soul if a few of the following descriptions apply to you:

- You can't sleep some nights because you are worrying about the days ahead.
- You rarely have a spring in your step or a smile in your voice, and the last time you had a belly laugh is a distant memory.
- You don't know the names of your colleagues' children or pets.
- You have travelled home at sunset and not even looked at the sky.
- You are in the habit of telling little white lies instead of confronting conflict.
- You no longer think about the gifts and talents you were passionate about when you were a teenager.
- You act on expediency rather than wisdom, and perhaps can't tell the difference.
- You typically lapse into superficial small talk with family and friends instead of discussing significant matters.
- You can't listen all the way through a favourite song or piece of music without getting fidgety.
- You are horrified by the thought of walking alone on a beach for an hour of reflection and contemplation.
- You have thought about sponsoring a child from a developing country for years but never got around to it.
- Or you have never thought about helping a developing country or even helping your local community when it is in need.

If being "rich in soul" equates to having internal well-being, inner calm, wholeheartedness, contentment, finding warmth from the people in your life, satisfaction from a higher purpose in your heart, a spring in your step, refreshment of spirit – and the good ol' Christmas trilogy of love, joy and peace – then answer the following question:

How "soul-rich" do you feel?

Not rich in soul at all	1	Dead soul
	2	Survival-mode soul
	3	Satisfactory soul
	4	Growing soul
Very rich in soul	5	Enriched soul

So how much do you need to read this book? Take your "time-poor" score and add it to your "soul-rich" score and see how you rate in the table below. This, of course, is a completely unscientific analysis – but it may shed some light!

How did you score?
Add up the two numbers you have chosen and consider the following suggestions:

Scoring 2–4	Keep reading because you are in serious need of some help! You either need more time in your life or a major refreshment to your soul.
Scoring 5–7	You seem to be doing "just OK". If you feel there is room for improvement (especially regarding the state of your soul), then you will find encouragement in these pages.
Scoring 8–10	Congratulations! It sounds like you are doing really well in the soul-enrichment stakes. So when you have finished reading this book, perhaps consider gifting it to a friend in need.

Quick Guide to Reading This Book

If you are particularly low on the time-poor scale, then I appreciate that reading this book may be a practical impossibility! Apart from reading when commuting or on the loo, or a chapter each night before you sleep, I suggest you check out the Contents or the following "quick guide" and dip into those chapters which might add some value in the shortest possible time.

Part A of the book explores 16 potential casualties of a busy life. When we neglect these aspects of life it can lead to numbness in our souls, but when we nourish them they can be pillars of our soul enrichment. These 16 aspects of life can be divided into four main spheres, with each sphere encompassing four qualities:

4 spheres	16 soul enriching casualties of a busy life			
People Around Us	Generosity Chapter 2	Sociability Chapter 3	Unity Chapter 4	Intimacy Chapter 5
World Around Us	Beauty Chapter 6	Equity Chapter 7	Opportunity Chapter 8	Adversity Chapter 9
Ourselves Internally	Clarity Chapter 10	Serenity Chapter 11	Vitality Chapter 12	Spirituality Chapter 13
Ourselves Externally	Creativity Chapter 14	Integrity Chapter 15	Levity Chapter 16	Love Chapter 17

Some of us are better at engaging with one or another of these spheres, although an extreme workaholic may find themselves neglecting all four. So when reading this book, it may be efficient to focus purely on the areas where you know you are most in need. Alternatively, you can just dip into each of the chapters to get a taste of the impact that different casualties might have.

Apart from telling the real life stories of women who have struggled to maintain a rich soul in the context of a time-poor life, each chapter has a series of "60 second solutions" and "lengthier remedies" – both of which suggest ways we can re-engage with a particular neglected aspect of life with minimal expenditure of time. I appreciate that a time-poor professional woman often does not have the space to re-engage easily with these casualties, and you might well ask, "What can possibly be achieved in 60 seconds?" The answer is simple: there is little point in my suggesting to a busy person in survival mode that the answer to a deadened soul is a day-trip to the beach or a six-month sabbatical. Instead I am proposing we start with some very easy remedies – things that can be achieved in less than one minute but can still have an impact on rejuvenating our souls.

There is no intention that you should treat the "60 second solutions" like homework. Rather, the lists are there as reminders of various strategies you can use throughout the day to make a difference. Alternatively, you may decide to approach things in a methodical way – for instance, you could respond to the "60 second solutions" by:

- choosing one or two to action each day
- focussing on one *type* of solution for a number of days in a row (such as those in the category "Recall Significant Incidents")
- deciding to work your way through the ideas for one particular casualty over a month or two.

The "lengthier remedies" range from five minutes to one hour and beyond. Many of them will be made more efficient through deliberate forward planning. In fact, it can easily take less than 60 seconds to make a plan which later leads to a "lengthier remedy". One way of responding to the lengthier remedies is to resolve that you will try to action at least one every month.

Part B of the book explores some issues that might become obstacles to our pursuit of a rich soul. Sometimes we are responsible for our own predicament, and sometimes life does not go according to plan and external factors intervene. There are four key dilemmas we might face at different moments in our lives:

Obstacles to soul enrichment

What if we self-sabotage our soul enrichment by letting our more pesky personality traits get the better of us?	Chapter 18
What if our lives are out of kilter with our values and beliefs about ourselves, our work and the world around us?	Chapter 19
What if things go bad and we are distressed by suddenly being out of a job and having lots more discretionary time than usual?	Chapter 20
What if we are asking the wrong question, and we've tried everything, and we still have no peace on the inside?	Chapter 21

These four chapters shed light on these obstacles and explore ways we can move forward.

PART A

❧

Reclaiming Sixteen Casualties of a Busy Life

Re-engaging with the People Around Us

It is not uncommon to neglect the people around us when we are incredibly time-poor. It is far too easy to stop being generous to others, and often we start to avoid being sociable altogether. We can also fail to appreciate the community in which we live and the benefits of unity amongst us all. Another casualty of being busy is that we can settle for shallow instead of close relationships with our loved ones.

These four casualties of a busy life – Generosity, Sociability, Unity and Intimacy – can be unmistakably soul enriching if not neglected. The following four chapters provide ideas on how to re-engage with the people around us, and so to enhance life for both ourselves and others in the process.

"We mostly focus on the good giving does for others – the good it does for
our community. But just as profound is what it does for us.
Because it is really true that while we grow physically by what we get,
we grow spiritually by what we give."[1]
Arianna Huffington

"...if some deed of mercy or generosity meets our eye, what
reverence and love does it inspire! Do we not say to ourselves,
'I should like to have done that myself'?"[2]
Jean-Jacques Rousseau

Chapter 2

ॐ

Generosity

MOST OF US HAVE HEARD that it is better to give than to receive, and I am sure that most of us actually believe this principle is true.[3] But how often do we act on this? It is easy to neglect being generous and kind when we are busy. And accordingly we fail to bring a benefit to others, and we forfeit the sense of inner gladness that accompanies acts of generosity.

Rebecca

Rebecca is a corporate lawyer who unexpectedly ended up in court herself. She has had to weather many legal storms during her career, but in this particularly dark period (when her corporation was being investigated and her role in the company was being scrutinised), Rebecca had three months when she barely saw her husband and three children. She was working seven days a week – usually in the office from eight o'clock in the morning to eight at night, and working again when she got home. She was under-resourced and exhausted during these months, but the constant pressure of having to prepare for and appear in court day after day meant she did not have any space in her life.

Time Poor Soul Rich

However, there was one thing Rebecca found relaxing, and somehow she made time for it each Saturday morning. She loved to cook. For her it was not so much about being creative in the kitchen but about providing a feast for her family or friends. She used the cooking of food as a way to bless others. It was the expression of her generosity – and it not only blessed others but also enriched her at the same time.

Rebecca's mother is of Slovenian descent, and food was always central to her European way of bringing the family together. Rebecca inherited the "cooking gene" from her mother, and she loved to use this gift to provide food for others. And not just any food but wonderfully satisfying and interesting food! So even when her corporation was being dragged through court (and she with it), Rebecca made time for an act of generosity – cooking a feast for her family on a Saturday.

> "The generous soul will be made rich, And he who waters will also be watered..."[4]
>
> *King Solomon*

At another less stressful time in her career, Rebecca was planning to visit a partner from a law firm who had a new baby. She was not sure what would be a suitable gift for this successful and wealthy woman. She decided to make a lemon tart – and the gift was so warmly received (the woman was overwhelmed with gratitude) that Rebecca continues to this day to give gifts of home-cooked food to anyone in need.

Lynette

Lynette's expression of generosity reflects a completely different level of commitment. Lynette has always been time-poor, juggling her job as a senior member of staff at a private school with assisting her husband in an overseas export business.

Years ago, Lynette's sister was crippled by drug addiction, and when she had a baby she could not care for him. Lynette and her husband adopted the child. Lynette would say that it was the most natural thing to do, but it certainly changed the course of her life, and also the life of her husband.

In more recent years, Lynette has also opened her home to her mother, who lives in a self-contained unit attached to the house. This

16

would not seem unusual in many cultures where the extended family generally lives together for life, but in the West the opening of one's home to others (be they family or stranger) is now seen as quite a rare gift. Lynette would maintain that having her mother in her home is only good for the family and not a burden.

Diana

Diana is a busy professional mediator. However, she and her husband donate a Saturday four times a year to a local church initiative which gives respite to the carers of children with disabilities. They take the children out for the day and help them experience different adventures, such as a visit to the aquarium or the zoo, or going rock climbing or bowling. Diana says that these children are a blessing to her, but she also sees the children getting joy from coming together in these outings. (There is more of Diana's story in Chapter 4.)

Charlotte

There are now whole websites associated with ideas for "random acts of kindness" (RAKs). People across the world are clearly convinced that kindness and generosity are soul enriching activities.

Charlotte's husband died of a brain tumour when their second child was only a newborn, so she has always had to juggle to survive. She works full-time for the government, and she is involved with nearly ten community organisations or clubs where she has three different leadership roles. Charlotte attends church once a week (and is on the rosters for flowers, prayers, reading and counting the offering), and she regularly sings in a choir.

Despite being chronically time-poor, Charlotte is someone who always tries to be prepared for RAKs. She carries a spare train ticket in her pocket in case a homeless person asks her for help to travel, and if she is asked for money for a meal, she ducks into the nearest cafe to buy the person some food. Charlotte is a true "gift giver". She is always thinking about the gifts she can give to others, and she actually keeps a scrapbook where she pastes pictures of potential gifts that she wants to remember for the future.

Another technique that Charlotte uses to help with her giving is to sit down on the day she gets her tax return to calculate how much money she will be donating to organisations in the following year. Charlotte then lists the organisations she wants to support and sometimes writes to them to seek clarification on their use of donations. She then preferences those who actually write back!

Giving of ourselves without expecting anything in return is true generosity – be it financial or some other gift. For the time-poor professional woman, sometimes a financial gift is the easiest method of expressing generosity.

Anne

When I started my legal recruitment business, I resolved as one of my mission statements that when the company was suitably profitable we would sponsor a disadvantaged woman to study law. At the end of my third year in business, we could finally meet this goal. My company donated the money to sponsor four women in the Middle East to study for their law degrees. This gift has been very rewarding for me and my staff – and all it took was a vision, some research and a bank transfer.

My next goal is a donation for a woman from Rwanda. Until recently, Rwandan widows and their children were left destitute when the man of the family died – traditional law did not provide for the widow to inherit. Instead, the husband's family would come and reclaim any property, and often the widow and her children were left out on the streets. Even though the law has now changed, many women in Rwanda are not aware of their legal rights. There is a great need for women lawyers who are able to educate other women regarding their rights to inherit property. Female lawyers will also be able to teach families about the advisability of couples preparing wills with instructions about who should inherit. A small financial gift from the other side of the world is a large contribution towards an African woman becoming a lawyer.

❧

Despite the wealth in many Western countries, research has shown that "wealthier people are less likely to be generous and give to charity".[5] It is the people from poorer socio-economic backgrounds who are known to give more selflessly. This research is explored in Anne Manne's book about narcissism in modern society, and she says that "the richer a person is the meaner they are".[6] The research did reveal an interesting exception to this trend. When wealthy people had recently been exposed to a video showing disadvantaged people in need, they did increase their generosity. There is a lesson here that we need to stay informed about the well-being of those who are less fortunate than ourselves!

> "The best part of life is not just surviving, but thriving with passion and compassion and humour and style and generosity and kindness."[7]
>
> *Maya Angelou*

Arianna Huffington, co-founder and editor-in-chief of the *Huffington Post*, wrote her book *Thrive* after collapsing from exhaustion and lack of sleep in 2007. She woke up in a pool of blood because she cracked her head on her desk on the way down. This event was the catalyst for her to do a lot of soul searching. When she started examining the lives of those who were truly thriving, Arianna concluded that they made room for "well-being, wisdom, wonder, and giving".[8] Arianna explored these qualities of life, and she is convinced that "giving" is something we will all find soul enriching.

Just as we enjoy it when others are generous and kind to us, so we bless others when we are generous and kind to them. And, of course, our soul is enriched along the way.

60 Second Solutions to Re-engage with Generosity

1. *Recall Significant Incidents:*
   - From your childhood, think of a time when someone's generosity really blessed you. Ponder how you can bring a similar blessing to others.
   - From your current experience, consider how you feel when you sacrificially give money, gifts or service and time to someone. Reflect on what other opportunities exist to give gifts.

2. *Review Your Workplace:*
   - Find moments when you can express generosity or random acts of kindness.
   - Praise or encourage those around you when they achieve good things.
   - Share your snacks with a colleague.
   - Look for opportunities to open a door for a colleague or to make them a cup of tea or coffee.
   - Ask if anyone needs anything if you are heading out near a shop.
   - Liaise with your business to give a proportion of seminar fees or some other income to a charity of the company's choosing.

3. *Resolve for the Future:*
   - Decide what percentage of your income you are going to give to others in need.
   - Decide when you are going to make those donations and set an electronic reminder so you don't forget.
   - Decide to create a "giveaway box" at home in which you deposit clothes, food and other items which can then be given to someone in need.
   - Decide if you want to (or are able to) commit any time in the future to assisting with a local charity (such as a soup kitchen).

4. *Research and Imagine:*
    Search the internet for information on:
    - worthy charities to donate to
    - random acts of kindness
    - how to give blood
    - the location of current famines in the world
    - the location of current natural disasters in the world.

5. *Record in Your Notebook or on Your Electronic Device:*
    - Write a list of those causes you want to donate to.
    - Write a list of those family and friends you want to bless with an act of generosity.
    - Record your future goal in relation to donating your time to a worthy cause.
    - Save pictures or photos of things that you would like to give as gifts to others.

6. *Reach Out to Others:*
    - Contact a local church or mission organisation to see what their current highest priority is for donating goods or money.
    - Give a flower, a compliment or a smile to a stranger who looks sad.
    - Identify someone in your local area who needs assistance and ask what they need.
    - Next time you see a person begging for money to buy food, take them into the nearest shop and buy them something to eat.
    - Choose a book that you once enjoyed, and order a spare copy online to give to someone who will benefit from it.
    - Give up your seat on public transport for someone less able than yourself.

7. *Refocus with a Time-Poor Prayer:*
    - Thank you God that you are a generous gift giver. Thank you for the gift of forgiveness. I would love to be more generous in

my life. I would also love not to feel guilty all the time. Please help me find the way to leave guilt behind me, and help me give generously to others. Enrich my soul.

8. *Rest for 60 Seconds:*
   - Stop everything; think of an act of generosity you are grateful for right now; and rest in the knowledge that you can be free from guilt.

Lengthier Remedies

- Buy or make a gift for a friend.
- Sponsor a poor child in a developing country.
- Sponsor the university studies of a woman in a developing country.
- Donate a small business loan for a fledgling business in a developing country.
- Donate some "pre-loved" business clothes to an organisation that provides clothes for disadvantaged women.
- Drop off some spare food, drinks, new underwear or children's gifts to a local homeless shelter.
- Visit an elderly friend who can't get out much.
- Facilitate assistance for someone in your local area who is in need.
- Watch the movie *Babette's Feast*.
- Read *What's So Amazing about Grace?* by Philip Yancey (Zondervan, 1997).

"We are born helpless. As soon as we are fully conscious we discover
loneliness. We need others physically, emotionally, intellectually;
we need them if we are to know anything, even ourselves."[9]
C.S. Lewis

"Two are better than one, because they have a good reward for their toil.
For if they fall, one will lift up the other; but woe to one who is alone
and falls and does not have another to help. Again, if two lie together,
they keep warm; but how can one keep warm alone?
And though one might prevail against another, two will withstand one.
A threefold cord is not quickly broken."[10]
An Ancient Jewish Teacher

Chapter 3

❧

Sociability

STUDIES IN HAPPINESS HAVE SHOWN that we need other people for our well-being. Social isolation is said to be just as likely a factor in illness or early death as things like high blood pressure, obesity and smoking.[11] Of course, if you are an introvert, then catching up with crowds of others will not bring you great joy – yet even introverts are enriched through contact with their friends. I am not talking about the intimacy explored later in this section but about the lighter social contact that forms part of being in a community.

I regret that too often I have neglected my friends. It has been nice to think about catching up with some of them over a relaxed dinner, but then a whole year has passed and I have failed to follow through. I've been too busy and too tired. I have even been known to plan on diarising a series of friend-encounters, and then found myself too preoccupied to get around to putting anything in my calendar.

When we are time-poor, it is highly likely that socialising with others will become a casualty unless we plan ahead and at least try to schedule a date.

Elizabeth

Elizabeth is a procurement manager for a large corporation in Melbourne. When stretched for time she has had to abandon being a "super hostess" in order to stay in touch with her friends. This was particularly true when the illness of a colleague left Elizabeth solely in charge of completing and submitting a tender application. She got very little sleep that week as she had a five-day deadline to complete the lengthy documentation. Some nights she was up until 3.00am drafting the tender, and some mornings she was up at 4.00am proof-reading the same. She barely had a spare moment that week, but she did make time for one small event.

Weeks earlier, Elizabeth had arranged for a group of friends to come to dinner on the Thursday night (not knowing she would be landed with the full burden of completing the tender). Instead of cancelling the dinner, Elizabeth contacted her friends and explained the situation. She told them she would love to see them, but that there would only be time to meet for 90 minutes, and they would need to bring the food. Rather than forfeit the event, Elizabeth realised that meeting with her friends over a brief dinner would bring some lightness to an otherwise heavy week. And she had to ignore her desire to be perceived as a "super hostess" by letting her friends know she needed help.

> "There is nothing better than a friend, unless it is a friend with chocolate."[12]
>
> *Linda Grayson*

Elizabeth's gift for being hospitable was evident even when she was young. As a teenager she remembers being at a party where there were 20 women and barely any men. After visiting a shop to buy supplies, Elizabeth saw a male friend from her hostel, and before long she had managed to secure 17 new male party guests to help with the numbers.

One of Elizabeth's current strategies to maximise her chances of extending hospitality to her friends is to always cook a double measure when she is preparing food, and then to freeze the spare meal for later. Elizabeth is also quite strategic about diarising different friends she is planning ahead to invite to dinner. She finds that if she thinks ahead about a future dinner party – including which of her friends will mix well with others, and what food she will serve – then such an event is far more likely to happen. She also has an ongoing appointment at 6.30am every morning with one or two friends who live in the same building complex. They walk together for up to an hour, and if an older, less-mobile friend is available, they stop for a cup of coffee at a cafe in the park to allow her to join them.

Elizabeth's desire to be sociable is not just confined to her friends. She also loves to help her son and daughter-in-law by babysitting her two grandchildren whenever she can. Elizabeth has managed to combine her generosity to her children, the development of intimacy with her grandchildren and her love of beauty and creativity by introducing her grandsons to the art galleries of Melbourne. At ages three and six, this is quite an ambitious exercise, but it certainly provides joy to Elizabeth at a number of levels. She has also tried to keep in touch with her son by calling ahead to see if he is free for a quick cup of coffee as she is passing his office on her way to work.

Bec

Bec is married without any children. However, her role as a teacher of children with special needs has meant she has always been surrounded by youth – many with intellectual disabilities and associated behavioural problems. Bec gets to the school between 8.00 and 8.30am and she hopes to leave by 5.00pm, but often it is later. She loves her work, and her day-to-day world involves relating to a broad group of colleagues, parents and students.

Despite relating to large numbers of people every day, one of the highlights of Bec's week is catching up with friends or family to chat. She might go with a group to a movie and then debrief over coffee, cake and a chat. Bec loves to attend a church home-group one evening a week, to explore new insights about God and to chat. And she loves to spend time with God and – you guessed it – to chat. One of her strategies to gain a little more time in the morning which allows her the space to have her God-chats is to eat her breakfast in the car. She has a specially designed car container for porridge!

Milly

After having an unplanned pregnancy at the age of 40, Milly spent time in a psychiatric hospital. She had already given up her job as a social worker because she was completely burnt-out, but unexpectedly she then had the stress of a new infant and a lurking mental illness. However, Milly slowly restored her sanity and began to re-engage with others.

> "I would rather walk with a friend in the dark than walk alone in the light."[13]
>
> *Helen Keller*

One of Milly's coping mechanisms was to once again rub shoulders with others in the community. Milly got involved with the school council; she helped manage the netball team; she contributed to working bees and fetes for the school; and she organised morning teas to raise money for breast cancer. Milly had not found time for any of these pursuits when she was working full-time in social work, but returning to such relationships was restorative to her soul. (There is more of Milly's story in Chapter 17.)

❧

One of the characteristics of the twenty-first century that has fundamentally changed the way we relate to one another is the widespread revolution in communications technology and social media. There is evidence to suggest that an intense use of Facebook has a correlation with increased levels of loneliness. There is also the suggestion that online relationships have a tendency to be increasingly detached rather than increasingly meaningful.[14] However, we can equally appreciate that these modern technologies provide convenient and speedy ways for us to stay in touch with others.

So rubbing shoulders with friends and acquaintances in the flesh can be a great way to bring some joy. When we are old and frail, business and paid work will be only memories, but people will be the ones standing by our bedside. And even though a video call cannot squeeze a sick person's hand, it can still be comforting to see the face of a family member or friend who cannot be present. So when we are time-poor, we should not ignore online methods of staying in contact with others. A quick text message to touch base with a friend can be a welcome first step towards being sociable again.

60 Second Solutions to Re-engage with Sociability

1. *Recall Significant Incidents:*
   - From your childhood, what was one of the most enjoyable gatherings you recall, and why did you enjoy it? Ponder how to create a memorable gathering for some of your friends or family.
   - From your current circumstances, when was the last time you spent time with others (either one individual or a larger group) and found it soul enriching? Consider how to replicate this event.

2. *Review Your Workplace:*
   - Suggest a monthly social event.
   - Stop in the elevator or corridor to greet your colleagues and inquire after their welfare.
   - Smile and greet each person you see each day.

3. *Resolve for the Future:*
   - Decide to have a dinner party in the future.
   - Decide to go walking one day in the future, and resolve which friend you will ask to come along.
   - Decide to surprise a friend for their birthday with a special outing.
   - Decide ahead of time that you will have a girls' weekend away some time in the next year.

4. *Research and Imagine:*
   - Keep an eye out in your local area for good cafes in which to catch up with friends.

Search the internet for information on:
* quick dinner party recipes
* best dinner party games
* best theatre or musical shows coming to town
* best bushwalks in your area.

5. *Record in Your Notebook or on Your Electronic Device:*
   * Write a guest list for the dinner party you plan to hold; write some menu and table decoration ideas.
   * Write a list of the movies, concerts or theatre shows you would like to see, and make a list of the friends you intend to invite along.

6. *Reach Out to Others:*
   * Email a friend to suggest a lunchtime walk one day next week.
   * Contact a group of old university or school friends and suggest it is time for a reunion.
   * Call your best friend when between appointments or on the way home.
   * Exchange a friendly word with the shop assistants or public transport officials you interact with.
   * When your children, partner or friend interrupts you, stop for a moment. Turn to them, look them in the eye and ask what is on their mind. Then explain you have something to finish before you can assist.

7. *Refocus with a Time-Poor Prayer:*
   * Thank you God that you are not distant but want to relate to us all personally. Please help me to confide in you. Also, please help me to be hospitable to those around me, and help my friendships grow stronger. Refresh my soul.

8. *Rest for 60 Seconds:*
   * Stop everything; think of the friends you are grateful for right now; and rest in the knowledge that you are not alone.

Lengthier Remedies

- Organise and attend a monthly social event with colleagues at work.
- Have a dinner party and invite five friends.
- Go to the theatre or a concert with a few friends.
- Take a friend on a bushwalk or a stroll through a park.
- Buy a big box of chocolates and find someone to share them with.
- Read *Loneliness: Human Nature and the Need for Social Connection* by John Cacioppo and William Patrick (W.W. Norton & Co., 2008).

"Communities are not built of friends, or of groups of people with
similar styles and tastes, or even of people who like and understand each other.
They are built of people who feel they are part of something that is bigger
than themselves: a shared goal or enterprise, like righting a wrong,
or building a road, or raising children, or living honorably,
or worshiping a god."[15]
Suzanne Goldsmith

"For Christians, who believe they are created in the image of God,
it is the Godhead, diversity in unity, and the three-in-oneness of
God which we and all creation reflect."[16]
Desmond Tutu

Chapter 4

❧

Unity

MY FATHER TELLS ME THAT when he was young, the Protestant and Catholic boys threw stones at each other. Now in some countries there are Jews and Muslims fighting in the streets because of hostilities in the Middle East. This year as I write, Boko Haram terrorists in Nigeria have kidnapped more than 200 schoolgirls as "war booty"; ISIS militants in Iraq have beheaded foreign journalists, Yazidis villagers and Christians; warring bikie gangs continue to kill and maim each other; Ukrainian nationalists and Russian insurgents are in a civil war which resulted in the downing of a passenger jet, causing the deaths of 298 civilians; and the leader of North Korea, Kim Jong-un, allegedly continues to assassinate members of his uncle's family (including children) in order to be rid of any trace of his father's brother whom he had executed last year.

It seems the world is continually plagued by conflict (often with political, ideological or religious roots) and unity is far from prevailing. However, most people crave a peaceful existence, and those who find common ground with their neighbours usually find it enriching to the soul.

The word "community" is derived from an old Latin word meaning "things held in common", and there are many elements within our societies that unify us in enjoyable experiences. Consider, for example, zoos and botanical gardens: both are generally not-for-profit endeavours with the main purpose of preserving nature and enhancing the experience of life. Participating in such ventures can easily warm the soul. Who doesn't love the feeling of everyone joining together in a common pursuit or good cause? And yet such pursuits can easily be neglected when we are busy. I am not talking about the unity depicted by a mob-mentality, but about two or more people sharing a common idea or goal which is edifying and not harmful to others.

Natasha

Natasha had a wild and self-destructive youth in the entertainment industry, which is well known for its culture of sex, drugs and rock 'n' roll. After abandoning her entertainment job, Natasha married and had two children. She then spent quite a bit of time reflecting on what was really important to her and worked out that her true passion was for children and nature. She got a job at a centre for birds of prey, presenting flying demonstrations to visitors. She also developed shows for young children to bring them together in experiencing the falcons and owls.

> "One word can end a fight; One hug can start a friendship; One smile can bring Unity; One person can change your entire life!"[17]
>
> *Israelmore Ayivor*

Natasha found great solace and enrichment from working in the community with nature and wildlife. She loved to bring people together in these environments and help them open their eyes to the wonders of the natural world.

Eventually Natasha started volunteering as a tour guide at the local zoo. It gave her a thrill to see joy on the faces of those who were seeing animals up-close for the first time. Then she was successful in securing a role with the local parks agency – another major community initiative which unified people. She oversaw the environmental education programs for the parks, gardens and nature reserves.

Natasha was particularly pleased that the government was funding visits to the parks for poor and disadvantaged children. She knew that many of these children were not familiar with the pleasure that came from experiencing the beauty in nature, and she would ask them all to stop still, close their eyes and just smell their surroundings. Then she would get them to listen closely to what they could hear. And when they opened their eyes, Natasha would have some extraordinary plant or tree ready for their observation. These children experienced a sense of peace when they relaxed in the park.

Natasha's love of the natural world led her to study for a degree in zoology and environmental management while her children were still young. She describes this as a nightmarish period in her life. By then she was a single mother, and her daughter used to call her the "spaghetti mum" because she was "all over the place"! Being extremely time-poor meant that Natasha had little time to spend in her beloved garden, but she did find a great "60 second solution" to keep connected to nature around her home. She would take her cup of coffee onto the verandah and harvest the herbs for her kitchen, or water the plants, or take the dead heads off her flowering plants. This little engagement with nature took only as long as her morning coffee.

Natasha's love of nature had another rather unexpected outworking. She created her own religion – a "god-sprout" (tendrils in her mind that were connected to God) – because she could not find any religion she liked. She certainly did not want to have anything to do with the Christianity she had grown up with. Natasha was pretty satisfied with praying to her sprout. It came as a great surprise one day when the sprout talked back and told her to visit her old school chapel. She ignored this suggestion, but a little later in the day, when she was chatting with the sprout, again she felt encouraged to visit the chapel. Natasha could not understand it, but when the idea came to her a third time, she decided to see where it would lead.

Natasha expected the chapel to be locked, but it was not, and she expected it to be filled with people, but no one was there. When she sat down and looked at all the Christian paraphernalia, she immediately withdrew into herself. She decided to chat again with her sprout. But instead of having their normal conversation, something truly remarkable happened to Natasha. She felt God fill her with a loving, warming spirit. It was like getting an emotional, physical and intellectual blast from heaven. She found herself looking at the big empty cross above the altar and suddenly it made sense to her. She actually became a follower of Jesus that day (to her great surprise), and many years later, she still finds the unity in the Christian churches she has attended to be a great encouragement to her soul.

Diana

Diana (whom we met in Chapter 2) is a mediator, and she is a big believer in people trying to stand in each other's shoes. She gains great soul enrichment from bringing people together in a unified cause.

Being a mediator gives Diana many opportunities to facilitate peace and not war. Her cases range from bringing vexatious litigants to the table to hear each other's perspectives to resolving conflicts involving large groups of people.

One such case involved 30 apartment owners who could not agree on the fairest payment from each for services provided by the body corporate management. Each apartment was a different size, and some were closer to the common facilities of the centre courtyard than others on the outer edge of the complex. The apartments were initially constructed so that all owners paid the same fees. However, those who owned smaller apartments on the outside edge felt they should pay lower fees because the pool and gym facilities were more readily accessible to the inner circle of larger apartments.

> "Blessed are the peacemakers, for they will be called children of God."[18]
>
> *Jesus*

Diana wisely called a meeting of all owners at one of the smaller apartments (so those who were in the inner circle could see how far away their neighbours were). Eventually a compromise was reached.

It was agreed by all to reduce the fees of the outer apartments by a small margin, and the owners also agreed to create a couple of new doorways through common walls to facilitate more direct access to the centre courtyard and facilities. For Diana as a mediator, bringing a unified view to a previous warring community was a very pleasing outcome. For those in the apartment complex, the culmination of a unified approach was also very soul enriching.

Diana's earlier life did not bring with it nearly as much joy. In fact Diana, like Natasha, found herself unable to participate in the unity of the church for years. When she was first married, Diana was a regular church attendee, but after her second son died on Christmas Day at the age of seven months, Diana couldn't face returning to church – particularly at Christmas time, when everyone was celebrating the birth of Jesus with far too much good will and too many glad tidings. Her son had died of cot-death in his pram in their garden. Diana's grief was only magnified when she and her husband immigrated to Australia, and within months Diana found herself without a support network.

Diana still had her oldest son to care for, and soon a baby girl came along. But the family's troubles seemed to keep coming with her husband's business struggling, and with her having to return to full-time work in a local pharmacy before her daughter was two years old. As with all mothers who have small children, Diana was incredibly time-poor. Things were not made easier when finally her husband lost his business, they lost their house and they nearly lost their marriage. Then her daughter got pregnant at 15 and she was a grandmother!

During these years Diana read a lot about positive thinking, auras and other New Age concepts. None of this seemed to satisfy her, and eventually she started to feel that she needed God back in her life. Occasionally she attended church, but as soon as Christmas arrived she would stay home again.

After 16 years of not being able to face church on Christmas Day, Diana finally had a breakthrough. She was flipping through a children's Bible and found a definition of death which helped her thinking about her son. Diana felt as if God was speaking into her heart: "You can have joy on Christmas Day. Today is the day my son took his first breath on earth and it is the same day your son took his first breath in heaven." Diana's heart began to heal that day, and she and her husband are now actively involved in a local church community. They get great joy out of facilitating unity both in the church and the broader community.

☙

Desmond Tutu speaks of the African concept of *ubuntu*, which is the "essence of being human". He explains:

> *Ubuntu* reminds us that we belong in one family,
> God's family, the human family. In our African
> worldview, the greatest good is communal harmony.
> Anything that subverts or undermines this greatest
> good is ipso facto wrong, evil.[19]

Recognising what people have in common rather than searching for our differences can be a very edifying habit. There is joy to be found in that habit. One of the keys to pursuing unity is to examine the idea that we are all created equal, and to resist the superiority and prejudice that flows from a different worldview.

60 Second Solutions to Re-engage with Unity

1. *Recall Significant Incidents:*
   - From your childhood, think of one of the community events which impressed you because of the togetherness of everyone involved. Consider how that event was facilitated.
   - From your current circumstances, identify what local events or venues are creating unity amongst people and consider supporting one of them.

2. *Review Your Workplace:*
   - Find moments when you can draw attention to the common mission and vision in your organisation.
   - Defend someone who is being unfairly denigrated.
   - Encourage those who are in conflict to consider things from each other's perspective.

3. *Resolve for the Future:*
   - Decide to support a community event or activity which draws people together in a common cause.
   - Decide to always consider matters from the other side's point of view before taking a position.

4. *Research and Imagine:*
   Search the internet for information on:
   - conflict resolution skills
   - local botanical gardens
   - local open house events
   - local community projects
   - local church initiatives
   - win-win negotiations
   - acceptance, agreement and alignment.

5. *Record in Your Notebook or on Your Electronic Device:*
   - Write a list of the top tips for negotiating a win-win solution.
   - Write a list of the local community events and locations that you wish to investigate.

6. *Reach Out to Others:*
   - Contact someone who you know is being sidelined and give them some encouragement.
   - When you meet a new person, look them in the eye and repeat their name.
   - Contact a friend who lives near you to suggest you investigate a community project together.

7. *Refocus with a Time-Poor Prayer:*
   - Thank you God that you bring peace and unity to a world at war. Thank you that you let your own son become a human being so that he could live like one of us, and thank you that he always walked in step with you. Please help me follow his example and care for the marginalised in the world. And help me to respect those in my circle of influence. Enlarge my soul.

8. *Rest for 60 Seconds:*
   - Stop everything; think of some common ground you are grateful for right now; and rest in the knowledge that we are all in this together.

Lengthier Remedies

- Visit a local park, zoo, community garden or other community venture.
- Get involved in a local community or church initiative – for instance, visiting people in hospitals or prisons or celebrating Christmas at a carols evening.
- Work on the mission and vision statements for your workplace.
- Do a course in win-win negotiations.
- Join a local sports club and become part of a team.
- Read *God Is Not a Christian: And Other Provocations* by Desmond Tutu (HarperCollins, 2011).

"Digital intimacy ruins the appetite for the real thing. So when kids are gaming or even when spouses are gaming, they lose their appetite for genuine intimacy...for getting their intimacy needs, their hunger for significance and attachment, with the family..."[20]
Gordon Neufeld

"If you age with somebody, you go through so many roles – you're lovers, friends, enemies, colleagues, strangers; you're brother and sister...That's what intimacy is, if you're with your soulmate. Marriage is a risk; I think it's a great and glorious risk, as long as you embark on the adventure in the same spirit."[21]
Cate Blanchett

Chapter 5

❧

Intimacy

WHEN A VICE-CHAIRMAN of Warburg's Bank was asked what he believed to be the greatest casualty of a busy life, his response related to "intimacy".[22] So who are we neglecting when we are busy? Our partner? Our children? Our parents? Our best friends?

Even when I do see my friends, I am often guilty of having shallow relationships. It still saddens me that one Christmas, after I had travelled all the way to Adelaide to see my family, Christmas Day came to an end and I had not managed any deep and significant chats with anyone. I realised afterwards that with better forward planning to be meaningful in each of my conversations, I might have gone home feeling I had connected with my family rather than just having said hello, hurrah and goodbye!

Susan

Susan has been a barrister in Melbourne for around 20 years, and over that time she has become very creative about maintaining close relationships with her husband and three children. Having come from a family where her father was absent from the time she was a baby, Susan has always put a strong priority on forging intimacy with her own family. She believes intimacy comes from feeling wanted and needed, and when she greets her partner or children in the evening, she tries to make it a joyful and appreciative hello.

In order to plan ahead and create some free time for her children when they were young, Susan would "block out" most days in every school holiday period, not accepting legal briefs requiring work at court on those days (although she would work from home if needed). When not working, she would try to be "in the moment" with her children –

> "...there's nothing more intimate in life than simply being understood. And understanding someone else."[23]
>
> *Brad Meltzer*

whether at the park, bowling alley, library or footy game. Susan tried not to be distracted by email when spending time with her children.

When her children were back at school, Susan would be faced with urgent and difficult trial work that gave no respite for days or weeks at a time. During these seasons of stress, she could be busy until 10.00pm and then rise at 4.00am to start work again. Despite this

workload, Susan was still committed to connecting with her children and her husband. She set up a home office so she was accessible to the children, and if they came to her with a question, she always put down what she was doing to look them in the eye and listen.

When they were young, she gave them writing or drawing projects to do while she worked nearby. It became a tradition at the start of the school holidays to take the children to a craft store, haberdashery shop or hardware store and let them buy whatever they wanted (within a budget); the children would then take their treasures home and be creative with them for hours, working near her. As they got older, Susan would work alongside them as they did their homework.

One of the ways Susan connected with her 11-year-old daughter when her job was particularly consuming was to work from her home office and send her daughter away to prepare a menu for an imaginary "sunshine cafe". When her daughter presented the menu, Susan selected her meal and gave her daughter the money to buy the ingredients. Her daughter then spent a happy afternoon cooking, and eventually presented the meal to her mum just in time for dinner. And, of course, Susan paid for her meal according to the price on the menu, and her daughter dutifully and happily cleaned up the kitchen. For Susan, this was a fun way to interact with her daughter, encourage her newfound love of cooking and keep her well occupied at the same time!

One day when she was feeling particularly disconnected from her teenage son, who could not be prised from his computer gaming, Susan took her work with her and asked if she could just "be with him" while he played. She happily worked alongside her son – being present but not interrupting – and when he was ready, the conversation flowed. Intimacy does not always require words. Sometimes just being in the room is enough. Susan has also found being in the car with her children is a great way to provide time for them to share confidences. Whenever possible, she will say yes to giving her children a lift, or accompanying them as they learn to drive.

Susan has always prioritised time with her husband – often through walks, coffees and dinners. When the children were smaller, she and her husband scheduled a weekly "date night". Even though the interruptions of life usually turned it into a fortnightly event, at least by planning ahead they knew they were prioritising quality time with each other. Another strategy used to protect their relationship is planning ahead for a day or weekend away without the children at least three times a year. Similarly, in order to keep strong relationships with some of her close friends, Susan also schedules a weekend away with "the girls" at least once a year. All of this scheduling is done well in advance, and helps her to manage her workload so it does not impinge on these prior commitments.

Susan is also a skilled diary "colour coder". She uses six different colours in her electronic calendar to represent her work, her personal commitments, her husband and each of her three children. This means she can easily see when events and obligations clash, and who is involved in each event. It also means she can try to ensure her work fits around special times with family and friends. Additionally, it helps her not to neglect her own well-being. Susan still tries to get to the gym regularly (and now her 16-year-old daughter goes along too, creating a new opportunity for intimacy); and she frequently goes for a 6.30am swim when she is up early preparing for court. Susan is a keen advocate of the "airline policy": if you don't fit your own oxygen mask first, you are not in a position to help anyone else!

One final strategy that Susan continues to use to create intimacy with her family is to outsource some of the tasks that would otherwise put strain on her relationships. Susan has a cleaner come once a week, and she employs a university student to do the "child transportation duties" after school, and sometimes to cook dinner. Susan learned long ago, when she was first persuaded to get a part-time nanny, that her kids did not mind who cooked their dinner as long as their mum and dad were there to eat it with them with smiles on their faces.

Susan has also learned the art of putting smiles on the faces of those around her by always trying to find the extra "magical moment" that she can bring to an event with one of them. For instance, when going to a movie with one of her children, Susan might suggest they dress up for the event, and then go to a special cafe afterwards to talk about the film.

Gayle

Gayle is a radiologist, mother of three and wife of a church minister. She and her husband have developed an interesting strategy to create stronger relationships with their teenage children. They aim to have the whole family sit down to dinner at the same time, and the goal is to have a discussion or conversation about matters of interest to the whole family. Then there are certain nights (particularly when on holiday) when the whole family will indulge in playing a board game together.

There is no doubt that a mixture of both real communication and arbitrary fun can create intimacy with others, and so enrich the soul. (There is more of Gayle's story in Chapter 12.)

Liang

Liang had very little space in her life when she was working at a global investment bank in Sydney. She would still be at work at 10.00pm most nights, and if there was a large transaction happening, it was not unusual for her to be at work until 2.00 or 3.00am. She often only saw her husband on weekends, and relating to him during the week was usually by phone.

However, apart from her husband, there was one other person Liang spoke to most days. She would try to ring her mother at least once a day – often in the taxi on the way home late at night. Sometimes this conversation was only for five minutes, and sometimes it was a lot longer – but the daily contact meant that her relationship with her mother remained intimate and not superficial. (There is more of Liang's story in Chapter 10.)

✎

Many would agree that human beings are more important than the work they are engaged in. When the World Trade Center came down in 2001, people were not asking "What businesses were lost in the buildings?" but "Who do you know who died in the collapse?" We naturally focus first on people and their destinies. So how do we maximise the chance of intimacy with those closest to us?

Brené Brown, an American researcher who has become well known for her work on vulnerability, has suggested that intimacy can be thwarted by feelings of shame, and that vulnerability can facilitate intimacy. She found that men, women and couples primarily overcome their issues through "honest loving conversations that require major vulnerability".[25] She suggests we have to be able to "talk about how we feel, what we need

> "Friends can destroy one another, but a loving friend can stick closer than family."[24]
>
> *King Solomon*

and desire, and we have to be able to listen with an open heart and an open mind. There is no intimacy without vulnerability."[26]

Brené's thoughts lead us to consider more carefully who it is we most long to be connected with. When we are intentional about the way we relate to our loved ones, we are more likely to experience the soul enrichment that is forged through intimacy.

60 Second Solutions to re-engage with Intimacy

1. *Recall Significant Incidents:*
   - From your childhood, what were your most intimate relationships and how did others make sure those relationships were strong with you? Ponder how you can use these strategies to strengthen your own relationships with your loved ones.
   - From your current circumstances, which people are you most connected to, and what has made these relationships strong? Consider how to maintain this intimacy.

2. *Review Your Workplace:*
   - Ask someone about themselves and really listen to their story.
   - Listen mindfully when a colleague tells you about their favourite sporting team, movie or pet, and make a point of remembering this information.
   - Suggest to someone that you have lunch one day to get to know each other better.

3. *Resolve for the Future:*
   - Decide to have a relaxed dinner or outing with a special friend.
   - Decide to schedule regular time with your top three "intimacy casualties".
   - Decide to always look for the extra magical moment you can bring to an event with a partner, child or friend.

4. *Research and Imagine:*
   Search the internet for information on:
   - best gifts for friends
   - how self-disclosure can increase intimacy with others
   - where to find the best home cleaners
   - where to find the best nannies or home childcare helpers.

5. *Record in Your Notebook or on Your Electronic Device:*
   - Write a list of the people closest to you, and plan how many times you would like to catch up with them in the next 12 months.
   - Write a list of the top five things you could share with others about yourself that would deepen your relationship with those friends.
   - Record the "snail mail" addresses of all your closest friends.

6. *Reach Out to Others:*
   - Send an edifying text message or email to your favourite person.
   - Contact a good friend you haven't seen in months or years and suggest it is time to catch up.
   - Write a short card or letter and send it by post to your favourite person.
   - Send out invitations for a private dinner with a special family member or friend.
   - When you greet your partner in the evening, deliberately kiss them for more than the requisite "short peck kiss".
   - When you greet your friend, deliberately give them a bear hug or a squeeze around the shoulders, rather than the requisite "air kiss".

7. *Refocus with a Time-Poor Prayer:*
   - Thank you God that you are the same yesterday, today and forever. Thank you that you have always wanted to be known by us. Please help me to get to know you, and help my relationships with those closest to me to be deepened. Please show me the way. Embrace my soul.

8. *Rest for 60 Seconds:*
   - Stop everything; think of somebody close to you whom you are grateful for right now; and rest in the knowledge that someone knows and cares about your inner self.

Lengthier Remedies

- Buy a special gift for a friend and deliver it with a card of appreciation.
- Purchase some gorgeous greeting cards and lovely writing paper, envelopes and stamps, and have them nearby to write to your special friends when you feel inspired.
- Hire a cleaner, nanny or part-time home helper to free up some of your time.
- Entertain a special family member or friend at a private dinner party.
- Attend a marriage or relationship strengthening course with your partner.
- Go to a special cafe after an event so you can debrief with your friends or family in style.
- Make a time to catch up with each of those who are closest to you, and share with them what you like or love about them.
- Read *Daring Greatly: How the Courage to Be Vulnerable Transforms the Way We Live, Love, Parent and Lead* by Brené Brown (Penguin Books, 2012).

Re-engaging with the World Around Us

IT IS EASY TO NEGLECT the world around us when we are consumed by work. With our head down immersed in our job, we can walk straight past something beautiful and not even give it a second thought. We can be vaguely aware of injustice somewhere in the world but do nothing to become informed or intervene. We can miss opportunities that might present themselves in front of our faces, and we can also forfeit personal growth by keeping our heads in the sand instead of facing adversity and conflict head-on.

These next four casualties of our busy lives – Beauty, Equity, Opportunity and Adversity – can also reinforce our well-being if not ignored. Following are some tips on how to re-engage with the world around us, and hopefully enrich our souls at the same time.

"The most beautiful people we have known are those who have
known defeat, known suffering, known struggle, known loss, and have found
their way out of the depths. These persons have an appreciation, a sensitivity,
and an understanding of life that fills them with compassion, gentleness,
and a deep loving concern. Beautiful people do not just happen."[27]
Elisabeth Kübler-Ross

"He has made everything beautiful in its time. He has also set
eternity in the human heart; yet no one can fathom what
God has done from beginning to end."[28]
An Ancient Jewish Teacher

Chapter 6

๛

Beauty

ONE OF MY MOST VIVID MEMORIES is of a breathtakingly beautiful sunset witnessed from the decks of a ship bound for Tasmania in the 1980s. I had a camera with me at the time, but as I went to "snap" the sunset, I made a conscious decision to put my camera away. I was overwhelmed by the desire to just drink in the beautiful view and give thanks for this majestic "stained glass window in the sky".

Somehow in a split-second I had realised that by photographing the sunset it would become "my picture", but by just admiring the sunset from the deck of the boat it could remain "God's picture". The sad reality of my current time-poor life is that I often don't leave the office until after dark, so I miss the sunset altogether; or more sadly, I am so preoccupied with my work that as I travel home I never give the sunset a second thought!

Don't get me wrong – I am in no way against photographing beautiful scenery. I am married to a man whose passion is photography, and I have photographed many sunsets since that trip to Tasmania. But strangely, the sunset I remember most fondly is the one I experienced with my camera in my pocket.

Actually, the skills of the great photographers and artists are essential for city-bound folk surrounded by cement and metal jungles.

It is quite refreshing to have in the office a painting or photograph of some breathtakingly beautiful scene from nature. A glassy reflective pond, roaring waterfall or vast ocean can all be delightful to our souls.

Human beings can also be "beautiful". Those of us who don't fit the classically beautiful mould portrayed in movies and magazines will probably be happy to focus on the "beauty within" – but there is also an "external beauty" that can bring joy.

Jacqui

Jacqui had always struggled with the usual stereotypes of personal beauty. She never felt she could be like the diminutive, angelic blonde girls who were always denoted as "pretty" from childhood. Jacqui had unruly dark brown hair, a large, strong frame and weight which always fluctuated. She ended up ignoring her appearance and dressing mainly in black clothes.

Jacqui was one of six women who graduated from her university in chemical engineering. Her first job as an engineer involved crawling around an oil refinery and inspecting equipment. In the world of engineering, a woman graduate is very noticeable, but Jacqui always felt "invisible", and she observed that people would commonly walk straight across her path as she made her way along the street.

"Art thaws even the frozen darkened soul, opening it to lofty spiritual experience."[29]

Aleksandr Solzhenitsyn

One day Jacqui heard about an online course which helped to identify your own personal type of beauty. After completing the course, she was like a new woman. She looked fantastic and had a newfound confidence. She started wearing bright, striking colour combinations and lots of fun, chunky jewellery. Her hair became a mass of waves, and she abandoned the traditional "straight styles" she had previously tried to apply to her unruly hair. Even better than looking her best, Jacqui also looked more peaceful and at ease.

Another change was that she no longer felt invisible in the street. Rather than rudely walking across her path, strangers were now more likely to stare at her and give her compliments. Jacqui was pleasantly surprised to find that paying attention to matters of external beauty had actually enriched her inner soul.

Marianne

Sometimes focussing on personal beauty can be downright painful instead of soul enriching.

Marianne always struggled with self-confidence because she was born with ectodermal dysplasia. This meant her hair and teeth never grew properly. Marianne's hair was thin and fair – more like a fine wispy web than normal hair – and her teeth were like pointy little puppy's teeth. (One of her sons had the same condition, and he was growing up with no teeth at all!) Marianne finally got corrective dental work around the age of 30, but it was another 20 years before she could muster the courage to wear a wig. Her self-image was just too broken.

Marianne is now usually seen in one of her groovy wigs, and many of her friends assume that her self-confidence increased when she began to cover her wispy hair in this way a decade ago. But Marianne claims the opposite is true. She says her confidence increased only after she got to know God better and stopped being mad at him. It was then that she felt brave enough to put on a wig. She certainly looks brilliant in her various hairdos, but she is just as happy throwing off her wig and wrapping a scarf around her scalp if it is too hot for extra hair. She has learnt to be content in her own skin.

There is no doubt that Marianne also has an inner beauty that all can see. Her current job is as a Lifestyle and Activities Coordinator with the elderly, and she is great at bringing cheer and brightness into the lives of those she cares for. Rather than raging at her creator for making her ugly, as she did for many years, Marianne now finds herself thanking God for making her who she is.

When I met Marianne, I was intrigued by her gift for surrounding herself with beauty – and her passion for the colour orange! She explains that her mother had lovely taste, always dressing elegantly and making her surroundings beautiful by coordinating the furniture in their home. Marianne inherited this eye for beauty, but somehow in her 20s she lost the ability to enjoy it. She had two small children and a husband who became increasingly abusive. When her marriage ended, she was shocked to suddenly notice she had decorated her home in dull cream and apricot hues. Marianne did not even find these colours attractive, and looking around her house gave her no joy (just as looking in the mirror made her sad).

Marianne is now around 60, looks great and makes a point of surrounding herself with things she finds beautiful. She loves vibrant colours, including reds, yellows, greens and her favourite, orange. Marianne has an orange car, an orange handbag, an orange couch, orange bed sheets, and orange pens and notebooks! When she makes a cup of tea in the morning, she always sets a beautiful tray (lime green to complement the orange cup and saucer) with matching plate, teapot and milk jug. She loves to relax for a few minutes with her toast and tea, enjoying the whole experience.

> "So much has been said and sung of beautiful young girls, why don't somebody wake up to the beauty of old women?"[30]
>
> *Harriet Beecher Stowe*

Marianne is pretty time-poor (and financially poor); she has always had to work a number of jobs to survive as a single mother. But even so, she keeps her eye on eBay so she can pick up a bargain here and there to improve her home. With little outlay of time, Marianne has been able to purchase a beautiful bathroom sink and some expensive tiles for a fraction of their cost by being a savvy shopper.

There is no doubt that Marianne gets great joy from surrounding herself with beauty, and from bringing beauty into the lives of others.

❧

When I was a child, I read Anne Holm's novel *I Am David*. David had grown up in a prison camp in Cold War Europe, and he had only known a grey, sad world of violence and deprivation. (In a weird kind of way, his grey world could be likened to that of a workaholic.) David had heard of the word music, but he did not know what it was. He had learned the words "nice", "lovely" and "beautiful", but he did not know how to use them.

When David escaped from the camp at the age of 12, he began a journey across Europe in search of a safe country. He tried very hard to blend in with local people, but there were too many things he just didn't understand. After being given refuge in someone's home, he was embarrassed to realise he had called the bathroom "lovely" when he should only have used the word "nice". And when asked to set the table for dinner, he shocked his host when he pulled out the most beautiful glassware and crockery and created a wonderful table setting – complete with a flower in a bowl at the centre. David had never seen such beautiful things, and he assumed it was normal to use them to make a table beautiful.

I had a similar but different experience during my sabbatical year at the age of 29. I was visiting a chalet in Switzerland called L'Abri, a home set up in the 1950s by a couple called Francis and Edith Schaeffer to allow people to come and explore the meaning of life, the universe and everything. The chalet looked out onto the Swiss Alps, and the staff had a policy of always decorating the dinner tables in a beautiful manner. If God had taken such care to create the beautiful mountains outside, they explained, then we should likewise make our surroundings beautiful.

The English poet John Keats wrote profoundly, "A thing of beauty is a joy for ever."[31] When we look around the natural world, there is plenty of beauty to satisfy our souls. It is certainly worth trying to bring that same abundance into our lives, our homes and our workplaces.

60 Second Solutions to Re-engage with Beauty

1. *Recall Significant Incidents:*
   - From your childhood, what is the first thing you remember that took your breath away because it was so beautiful? Ponder how to keep such beauty close in life.
   - From your current experience, what scenes from the world around you satisfy that part of you that loves beauty? Consider how to see these things more often.

2. *Review Your Workplace:*
   - Install a beautiful desktop picture on your computer (and mobile phone) and look at that picture now and again.
   - Place a beautiful sculpture or photograph on your desk or work wall (and look at that sculpture or photo now and again).
   - Buy or pick a flower to put in your office (and look at that flower every now and again).
   - Hang a beautiful picture or piece of artwork above your desk (and look at that picture or artwork now and again).
   - Affirm another colleague whose beauty is shining through, particularly if they are not the traditionally beautiful type portrayed in the media.
   - Play a YouTube recording of a beautiful piece of music.

3. *Resolve for the Future:*
   - Decide to look at – *really* look at – the trees, the sky, the clouds, the hills, the valleys, the wildlife and a rainbow or a sunset whenever you get the chance.
   - Plan to take an online course about dressing in a way that lets your beauty shine through.
   - Plan to take an exercise class to learn how wonderfully you have been made.
   - Decide that when you sit down to eat, you will put something beautiful on the table and light a candle.
   - Decide that when you buy a simple household or business item, you will purchase something you believe is beautiful as well as functional.
   - Decide not to "keep the best china for special occasions".

4. *Research and Imagine:*
   - Find a recording of a beautiful piece of music.
   - Find images of beautiful paintings; the most beautiful places in the world; most beautiful dogs; the most beautiful birds; the most beautiful architecture; the most beautiful fish, etc.

Search the internet for information on:
- dressing for your body type; dressing for your colouring; dressing for your energy type; dressing for your skin type
- what exhibitions or events are going to be in town (art exhibitions, pottery exhibitions, flower shows etc.) and list those are interested in.

5. *Record in Your Notebook or on Your Electronic Device:*
- Diarise the artistic exhibitions you would like to attend, and set some early reminder alerts.
- Take and keep photographs of beautiful things you pass every day.

6. *Reach Out to Others:*
- Contact someone who loves the same sort of exhibitions as you, and suggest that it is time you both chose something to attend.
- Contact someone who is seeking to let out their inner beauty, and arrange to get together to brainstorm strategies for change.
- Email a friend to suggest a walk in a park where you can admire the gardens.
- When you see something that looks beautiful, send a photo of it to a friend and entitle it "soul food".
- When you see a child doing a kind act, tell them how lovely it is to see their inner beauty in action.

7. *Refocus with a Time-Poor Prayer:*
- Thank you God for putting so many beautiful things in the world. You have a pretty awesome imagination. Please help me to appreciate the beautiful things I see, and please help me to create beautiful things myself, and to nurture my own beauty authentically. Make my soul shine.

8. *Rest for 60 Seconds:*
- Stop everything; think of something beautiful you are grateful for right now; and rest in the knowledge that a thing of beauty can be found in the most unlikely of places.

Lengthier Remedies

- Visit the museum or art gallery during lunchtime with a friend.
- Undertake an art appreciation course.
- Buy yourself some new clothes which better reflect your personality and your best colour tones.
- Give one room in your house a quick make-over to maximise its beauty.
- Go to a beautiful florist shop, smell the roses, enjoy the colours and textures, and buy a big bunch of flowers to put in your home or office.
- Read *Coastal Paradise Revealed* by Ken Duncan (Panograph Publishing, 2012).

"Dat little man in black dar, he say women can't have as much rights as men, 'cause Christ wan't a woman! ...Whar did your Christ come from? From God and a woman! Man had nothin' to do wid Him."[32]

Sojourner Truth

"Let not any one pacify his conscience by the delusion that he can do no harm if he takes no part, and forms no opinion. Bad men need nothing more to compass their ends, than that good men should look on and do nothing."[33]

John Stuart Mill

Chapter 7

꙰

Equity

In 1955 Rosa Parks, an African-American woman, was asked by a bus driver in Alabama to give up her seat to a white passenger because all the "whites only" seats had been filled. Rosa's refusal to stand-up led to her arrest. Martin Luther King Jr was soon leading a non-violent protest where black Americans refused to use the buses – the Montgomery bus boycott which lasted for 385 days – and this led to King's house being fire-bombed and him being arrested and jailed. Rosa Parks said it was not because her feet were tired that she stayed seated that day, but rather:

> …my soul was tired of being a second-class citizen. When I sat down and would not give up my seat, I was standing up for justice, for equality for all.[34]

There is a clear connection between justice and equity in the world and the wellness of our souls.

Most of us are familiar with the words: "The only thing necessary for the triumph of evil is for good men to do nothing." This quote is often attributed to Edmund Burke, but apparently it does not appear in any of his writings. However, it is a good paraphrase of things said by both him and John Stuart Mill (see Mill's comment above). I am sure we all believe it is important to keep our eyes on matters of injustice and inequity in the world, and to take action wherever possible. However, unless we work for a dedicated NGO (non-government organisation) fighting for the rights of a particular group in society, it is unlikely we have the time to consider matters of social justice in any great depth.

Meredith

Meredith has been working full-time for an NGO in Australia supporting community development programs in India. She absolutely loves her job, but even working in an organisation focussed on social justice does not guarantee you always appreciate the soul enriching aspects of what you are doing. Meredith has also been a board member on a youth-run organisation fighting poverty, and she admits she has a tendency to be "over-committed". She easily identifies with the feeling of being time-poor, and in order to remind herself of the soul enrichment that naturally comes from her job, she has placed a sticky note on her computer which reads: "I love my work; it's not just a job!"

"In true forgiveness there is freedom. Forgiveness says, 'These things that happened are all true, but in spite of them, I choose to forgive.'"[35]

Faith McDonnell

Meredith has always had a passion for social justice, and even before she took her current job she was looking for opportunities to be involved with matters of equity. This interest led her to study law, and when she left university she was offered a job in a top-tier national law firm. Meredith wondered if she would be "selling her soul". Fortunately, the law firm she joined had a strong pro bono program offering legal services to worthy recipients at no cost. Meredith very quickly volunteered to be involved in the pro bono and community engagement work, and later she became the lawyer who coordinated her Melbourne office's support of local NGOs and the staff volunteering program. She also started an environmental awareness program within the firm.

Eventually Meredith and her husband decided to take their passion further, and they both took a year of leave from their respective jobs and travelled to South Asia to volunteer with NGOs working in their areas of expertise. Meredith used her legal skills to help rescue vulnerable families who had been forced to work as slaves (some for their whole lives), and also to prosecute the business owners who had exploited them. This taste of working with marginalised communities spurred her on to find a job where she felt she was making an important contribution to the world, and when she returned to Australia, she secured her current NGO role instead of going back to the law firm.

As already mentioned, it certainly seems easier for a person to gain soul enrichment from their engagement with matters of equity if they are already working for an organisation focussed on social justice. However, Meredith actually provided ways for others to join in her vision by holding fund-raising events to assist with her trip to South Asia. Many people attended these events and learned about the growing problem of modern-day slavery and trafficking in Asia, and all were given the opportunity to financially support Meredith's work.

Rana

Rana is also a lawyer, but her career has taken a different path to Meredith's. Rana came to the law only after beginning her career as a social worker. Before working as a lawyer, she worked full-time in a shelter for homeless teenagers. She loved this work, but life was certainly challenging as she and her husband had their two small children living with them in the same dwelling as the homeless youth. Rana's father and grandfather were both lawyers, so eventually she gave in to her "genes" and returned to university to study law.

When Rana first practised law, she was involved with debt recovery disputes and drafting wills for clients. However, she now works representing the victims of assault by religious authorities. Rana's current law firm supports her working in a pro bono capacity, where her clients pay very little and, in some cases, nothing for her services.

She has been able to practise a "restorative justice" approach in this field, and she has found that she is enriched herself by having the privilege of helping her clients in their pursuit of justice and healing. (A completely different aspect in Rana's journey is described in Chapter 13.)

Anne

One of the ways I like to raise awareness of community development programs (and at the same time support them financially) is to give Christmas gifts to my clients which are a donation on their behalf to projects in developing countries. These gifts include chickens or goats purchased for families in need; tree planting and environmental care projects; safe water, sanitation and hygiene projects; and teacher training programs.

It is heartening to see the response of some of my clients who have decided to give the same sort of gifts to their friends. After all, who would not like to receive a goat or a pig (or at least the promise that one has gone to a good home at your expense)?

∽

Perhaps one of the most poignant examples of a busy time-poor professional woman neglecting matters of justice and equity is Adolf Hitler's secretary, Traudl Junge. Traudl was 22 when she became Hitler's secretary in 1943, and she was with him in the bunker right up to the time of his death. When she finally discussed her memories of working for him, she claimed to have been ignorant of the Nazi atrocities. However, she was clearly remorseful about never making inquiries to find out the truth. Traudl gave the following account of having her eyes opened after hearing of the Nazi war crimes during the Nuremburg Trials:

> I was satisfied that I wasn't personally to blame and that
> I hadn't known about those things. I wasn't aware of the

extent. But one day I went past the memorial plaque which had been put up for Sophie Scholl in Franz Josef Strasse, and I saw that she was born the same year as me, and she was executed the same year I started working for Hitler. And at that moment I actually sensed that it was no excuse to be young, and that it would have been possible to find things out.[36]

Sophie Scholl was a German girl whose Christian faith and strongly held political views led her to be part of an anti-Nazi resistance group called the White Rose. She was executed by guillotine at the age of 21, along with her brother Hans, after being caught distributing anti-war leaflets in Munich. Those who saw Sophie walk to her execution reported her courage. A couple of years earlier she had written, "How can we expect a righteousness to prevail when there is hardly anyone who will give himself up undividedly to a righteous cause?"[37]

> "...And what does the Lord require of you? To act justly and to love mercy and to walk humbly with your God."[38]
>
> *The Prophet Micah*

The lesson taught by Traudl Junge and Sophie Scholl is a sobering one. Some of us may spend the rest of our lives regretting that we did not open our eyes to injustice, and others of us may commit ourselves to a cause that leads to our own hardship, or even an early death, but with the blessing of a strengthened soul.

Maybe equity is best addressed when we remember that men and women can be both evil in their behaviour and triumphant in their pursuit of good. We all have a deep capacity for greatness and a wide capacity to stuff things up. But it certainly seems apparent we can be enriched (and contribute to the well-being of others) when we actively consider matters of justice and equity in our community and wider world.

60 Second Solutions to Re-engage with Equity

1. *Recall Significant Incidents:*
   - From your childhood, when did you first learn the meaning of injustice? Ponder how this can help you make a difference today.
   - From your current circumstances, what inequities are you aware of and which do you feel most passionate about? Consider how to get more involved.

2. *Review Your Workplace:*
   - Defend a colleague who is being unfairly criticised.
   - Suggest a business-wide sponsorship of a worthy cause.
   - Engage in discussions about business ethics.
   - Suggest that Christmas cards or gifts to clients can be donations on their behalf to community projects in developing countries.
   - Encourage the payment of a bonus or the provision of a flexi-day for someone who has given service beyond their brief.

3. *Resolve for the Future:*
   - Decide if there is a justice cause you want to take part in.
   - Decide if there is a social equity issue you want to stay informed about, and sign up to receive mail.
   - Decide that when you receive loose change, and there is a bowl for donations for an aid organisation, you will give away your spare change instead of putting it back your purse.

4. *Research and Imagine:*
   Search the internet for information on:
   - social justice issues
   - top NGOs in the world
   - world debt and jubilee programs
   - sex slavery and human trafficking in your country
   - abuse of animal rights in your country
   - forced marriage in your country
   - equal pay for equal work in your country

- inequality of education in the world
- community development program gifts and projects.

5. *Record in Your Notebook or on Your Electronic Device:*
   - Write the names and contact details for key people and organisations who are involved in the area of injustice you are most passionate about.
   - Brainstorm and record strategies of what you can do to make a difference in relation to some social cause.
   - Record the contact details for your state and federal Members of Parliament for future action.
   - Plan a letter or series of letters you want to send to various officials.

6. *Reach Out to Others:*
   - Contact an NGO you want to support and ask to be put on their mailing list.
   - Contact a friend with similar interests to yourself, and make a time to catch up for coffee or to attend an event in relation to the cause you are most passionate about.
   - Write a quick email to a politician to protest about or raise awareness of an issue.

7. *Refocus with a Time-Poor Prayer:*
   - Thank you God that I am not the final judge. Thank you that you are keenly focussed on both justice and mercy. Please help me to recognise and respond to injustice in the world. Please teach me what it is to have both grace and mercy, and help me not to be more judgmental than you. Sharpen my soul.

8. *Rest for 60 Seconds:*
   - Stop everything; think of some act of justice you are grateful for right now; and rest in the knowledge that God is a just judge.

Lengthier Remedies

- Attend an information seminar about an equity issue in your community.
- Become a committee member for a social justice organisation.
- Write a letter to your local Member of Parliament, informing them of an important issue and requesting that the government intervenes.
- Read *A Heart for Freedom: The Remarkable Journey of a Young Dissident, Her Daring Escape, and Her Quest to Free China's Daughters* by Chai Ling (Tyndale, 2011).
- Read *Girl Soldier: A Story of Hope for Northern Uganda's Children* by Faith J.H. McDonnell and Grace Akallo (Chosen Books, 2007).
- Read *Infidel: My Life* by Ayaan Hirsi Ali (Free Press, 2007).
- Read *My Forbidden Face: Growing Up Under the Taliban: A Young Woman's Story* by Latifa (Virago Press, 2002).
- Read *Slave: The True Story of a Girl's Lost Childhood and Her Fight for Survival* by Mende Nazer and Damien Lewis (Virago Press, 2004).

"I never lose an opportunity of urging a practical beginning,
however small, for it is wonderful how often in such matters the
mustard-seed germinates and roots itself."[39]
Florence Nightingale

"There is a tide in the affairs of men, Which, taken at the flood,
leads on to fortune; Omitted, all the voyage of their life Is bound in shallows
and in miseries. On such a full sea are we now afloat; And we must take the
current when it serves, Or lose our ventures."[40]
William Shakespeare

Chapter 8

❧

Opportunity

THERE HAVE BEEN VARIOUS MOMENTS in history when women's "opportunities" have been severely curtailed by cultural, religious or political interventions. In Afghanistan, women were not allowed to work, study or even leave the house without a male escort and a burqa (the head-to-toe covering with a small screen for the eyes) during the years when the Islamic Taliban were in government from 1996 to 2001.

In Australia, women who got married were required to resign from permanent jobs with the public service until the law was changed in 1966. During the Second World War, the "Women's Land Army" was active in the UK, USA and Australia, so that more men could be freed from jobs and go to war. Women also went to work in factories, often building munitions, aircraft and ground vehicles. After enjoying their diverse new jobs (and higher salaries) during the war years, many women were disappointed to lose them to the returning soldiers after the war ended.

But now we are in the 21st century, and most women have options – certainly in Western countries. We are often highly educated and can choose to do further study. We can work in professions that were traditionally only occupied by men, and we can choose to have babies. Of course, not all women can have children, not all women do further study and not all women can rise to the position of a CEO. But even so, the options for Western women today are more prolific than ever before.

There are two dilemmas we face in relation to opportunities in life: do we even see the opportunity in the first place; and if we do, should we take it? Being busy and tied-up with our current work makes both of these aspects difficult, and it means we can forfeit the soul enrichment that comes from pursuing a new opportunity or direction.

> "Sometimes opportunities float right past your nose. Work hard, apply yourself, and be ready. When an opportunity comes you can grab it."[41]
>
> *Julie Andrews*

I once head-hunted a lawyer who unexpectedly turned out to be over 70 years of age. He was very remorseful that he had worked at the same law firm for his whole career and it was now too late for him to move to another organisation. It seemed that throughout his life he had simply been too busy to review his situation and consider an alternative path. His work had consumed him for 50 years, and as a result he had never surfaced above his busy workload to consider any other opportunity.

Therese

Therese had more than a challenging career in nursing to keep her pre-occupied. She also had twin daughters and a husband who had been sick with heart disease throughout their marriage. But Therese loved her work as a registered nurse, and every time she got bored she looked around for a new challenge.

Therese just kept on learning. First she worked in neurosurgical theatre, then in aged care. Then she did pathology collection whilst studying a postgraduate qualification in midwifery. Next she went into post-operative care (she still remembers the time she had to miss the music awards night for one of her daughters because she was stopping a patient from dying). Therese's next challenge was to work with patients in iron lungs, and then she moved into rehabilitation and infectious diseases. Eventually she added a Bachelor of Educational Studies to her five postgraduate qualifications and went into nurse education.

It would have been easy for Therese to remain a bedside nurse and never progress in her career. But she found it inspiring and enriching to keep learning – and she hated being bored in her work. So for Therese, the technique of keeping one eye open for new opportunities became second nature. If the hospital she was working for was offering a course, then Therese generally applied to do it – even if it meant she then worked fewer hours and earned a little less.

Another technique Therese employed was to think ahead as to what skills she would like to have should her services be needed. Despite now being retired, she used her nursing experience to good effect on a recent trip to Kenya where she was able to assist with medical matters in an orphanage run by African nationals for local children.

Deborah

Deborah is another professional woman who has strived to excel in both her work and on the home-front. I was shocked when she told me which period of her life caused her to feel the most time-poor and depleted in soul. I had expected her to say she was most time-poor when her three children were young and she was juggling school-runs, home duties and full-time work as a partner at a national accounting firm. Unexpectedly, she said she has never felt as time-poor as she does now. Her three children have finished school, and they currently do their own laundry and take turns cooking the dinner – but Deborah nevertheless feels as if her soul has regressed into survival mode.

Deborah explained that she used to juggle things brilliantly when her kids were small – and she managed to handle her daily work tasks between 9.00am and 3.30pm in the office, finishing things later in the evening at home. Now that her kids are no longer at school, she can get to work at 8.00am or earlier, and in order to avoid the afternoon peak hour traffic, she has got into the habit of leaving after 7.00pm each night. Despite immensely enjoying her work, Deborah has come to realise she is no longer as efficient as she used to be.

Also, Deborah no longer has her soul enriching chats with the other mums at the school or her participation in the regular prayer group there. She is no longer running the youth group; no longer having open-house each Friday night for her children and their friends; no longer sewing kids' clothes and costumes; no longer indulging in cross-stitch. And she misses driving home in the daylight when she was able to appreciate the beautiful cloudy skies.

Deborah now has itchy feet, and she has recognised this as a sign that it is time to find a new challenge. She says that the best way for her to recognise an opportunity when it comes along is to pray first. She feels that if she has asked specific questions of God, then it is easier for her to notice the answers when they come.

✑

I have always remembered a piece of life-changing advice given to me and a group of fellow university graduates 25 years ago by Frank Brennan. Frank is a Jesuit priest, human rights lawyer, advocate for justice and reconciliation for the Aboriginal people of Australia, and the son of a former Chief Justice of the Australian High Court. Frank stood in front of this group of talented young professionals, and he warned: "You smart people will probably do well at whatever you put your hand to. But beware. If you say yes to everything, you will spread yourself too thin. It behoves us all to bow our knee before God, and ask him what we should put our energy into."

I gained another helpful piece of advice about direction in life from a missionary who always took two days or so at the start of every year to retreat and ask God what her priorities should be for the next 12 months. Her technique was to say to God: "Well, last year this is what I did. Should I continue with the same focus, or is there something new for me to prioritise in this coming year?"

I have tried to implement this advice for the last two decades, and I have to confess: it certainly helps me to know what to say no to! Because I do not have children, and because I have a law degree and run my own business, I frequently get asked to be on boards or committees – sometimes because of my skills, and sometimes because I am seen as "the requisite female on the panel"! By formulating ahead of time what my focus is to be for the year, I have frequently been able to decline requests to join this or that committee or board because I have another set of priorities. Equally, it becomes easier to recognise an opportunity that should be pursued if it is consistent with a predetermined focus.

However, just because a new idea comes out of left field does not mean we should ignore it. It is worth sleeping on any opportunity before saying no. Sometimes our circumstances can lead us to react negatively (or positively) before we have time to adequately assess the implications.

> "A desire accomplished is sweet to the soul..."[42]
>
> *King Solomon*

Finally, sometimes we have to go out and *make* an opportunity happen. If we are passionate about pursuing a particular thing, there is no harm in taking proactive steps to see it become reality. One of my favourite arts subjects at university was "History of Social and Political Ideas". After initially being told I was ineligible to enrol in the subject because it was only for a small group of third-year students (and I was still in second year), I negotiated hard to get myself into the course. I eventually won the right to enrol, and enjoyed learning about the history of liberalism, socialism, conservatism and feminism.

Sometimes opportunities are missed because we fail to notice them, but sometimes it is because we fail to pursue them. The key once we identify an opportunity is to have the wisdom to know if we should take it up. (There are further ideas about "clarity" in Chapter 10.)

60 Second Solutions to Re-engage with Opportunity

1. Recall Significant Incidents:
  - From your childhood, recall an occasion when you saw an opportunity and jumped up to grab it with both hands. Ponder why you could see it so clearly at that moment.

- From your current experience, recall an opportunity you said yes to that refreshed your soul, and ponder how to keep your eyes open for similar opportunities.

2. *Review Your Workplace:*
   - Find moments when you should put your hand up to take on a new project.
   - Recognise professional development and learning opportunities when they arise.
   - Recognise a likely mentor when they appear.
   - Block out a time in your diary which is purely a time to consider opportunities that might exist.

3. *Resolve for the Future:*
   - Decide to establish your key priorities on an annual basis so you have a framework in which to evaluate opportunities as they come up.
   - Decide ahead of time that you will cook (or purchase) an extra meal and have it in the freezer so it is easier to respond when the opportunity arises to invite someone to dinner.
   - Brainstorm the things you would like to achieve or experience in the next five or ten years.
   - Create a "bucket list" of the things you want to do before you retire or die.

4. *Research and Imagine:*
   Search the internet for information on:
   - wisdom about opportunities
   - techniques on making priorities
   - strategies on setting boundaries
   - best ideas to put on your bucket list.

5. *Record in Your Notebook or on Your Electronic Device:*
   - Write a list of your key priorities for the next 12 months.
   - Record the date you will go on a retreat to reflect on the coming year.
   - Write a list of the criteria by which you will evaluate opportunities as they emerge.
   - Write a list of opportunities that currently present themselves to you, for reflection and decision-making at a later date.

6. *Reach Out to Others:*
   - Contact the organisation or person who represents an opportunity you regret not pursuing.
   - When someone offers you an opportunity, don't say no immediately, but ask them to summarise the details in writing, and promise to consider it properly once you have their summary.
   - Contact a mentor or career consultant to suggest you catch up to review your future opportunities.

7. *Refocus with a Time-Poor Prayer:*
   - Thank you God that you see everything from the beginning to the end. Please direct my steps and prompt me to see opportunities when they arise, and give me the wisdom to know which to pursue. Guide my soul.

8. *Rest for 60 Seconds:*
   - Stop everything; think of an opportunity you are grateful for right now; and rest in the knowledge that tomorrow is not yet set in stone.

Lengthier Remedies

- Visit a recruitment consultant to review what options exist for your career going forward.
- Go on an annual retreat to reflect and set priorities for the coming year.

- Take up some postgraduate study in an area of interest.
- Read *What Colour Is Your Parachute? A Practical Manual for Job-Hunters and Career-Changers* by Richard Nelson Bolles (Ten Speed Press, revised annually).

"...character cannot be developed in ease and quiet. Only through experiences of trial and suffering can the soul be strengthened, vision cleared, ambition inspired and success achieved. Most of the men and women honored in history for their service to mankind were acquainted with 'the uses of adversity'."[43]

Helen Keller

"...and who sacrifices pleasure when it is within the grasp, whose mind has not been opened and strengthened by adversity, or the pursuit of knowledge goaded on by necessity? Happy is it when people have the cares of life to struggle with; for these struggles prevent their becoming a prey to enervating vices, merely from idleness!"[44]

Mary Wollstonecraft

Chapter 9

୨

Adversity

ADVERSITY IS AN UNLIKELY PILLAR of our soul enrichment. You may well be asking why you should invite adversity into your life. That's not what I am suggesting. But if we completely ignore or bury adversity and suffering rather than facing them head-on, we may well be poorer in soul instead of being strengthened and enriched.

It is easy to avoid any kind of conflict when we are busy. However, some crises cannot be avoided because they directly impact every aspect of our lives. There is also a different type of adversity – better described as an adventure – where we can be enriched by pursuing an activity that hones our endurance skills.

Julie

When Julie was 55, her husband suddenly died after dinner one night. She thought he was starting to laugh at the television, but an aneurysm was rupturing in his chest. He was only 63. Julie and her husband were still very much in love after 19 years of marriage, and even though her job meant she commuted regularly between Sydney and their home in Perth, they still stayed very close.

Commuting 4000 kilometres monthly to teach Management and Leadership at a Sydney tertiary institution had certainly meant Julie was time-poor. She and her husband spoke daily by phone, but to avoid the disconnection that time and distance create, they also developed a "21-day rule". They resolved they had to actually be in each other's company at least every three weeks (which sometimes meant her husband flew to Sydney to be with her) or otherwise they found they were no longer properly connecting. Instead they would just end up "gliding across the headlines". But suddenly it all came to an end when Julie's husband was gone.

Only one week later, Julie was being sued by her deceased husband's business partner. A plan for her husband to buy out his partner for $8 million had not proceeded due to his death, and Julie was now being prevented from having any involvement in the business. She spent the next year trying to come to terms with her grief, the settlement of over $16 million in debts, and a judicial system that seemed to be outwitted by her husband's business partner. She was even more time-poor than she had imagined possible.

"There is in every true woman's heart a spark of heavenly fire...which kindles up, and beams and blazes in the dark hour of adversity."[45]

Washington Irving

In order to create some light at the end of her tunnel, Julie planned a trip with friends to visit Machu Picchu in Peru. While her friends went trekking for a few days, Julie stayed behind to spend some serious time on her knees. She felt she needed to find some answers, and she earnestly prayed to God for guidance about her future.

After three days of storming the heavens, Julie felt she had some direction. She was convinced she should resign from her Sydney job and move to Melbourne where her daughter Alison, son-in-law and grandson lived. Her grandson was only three years old, and Julie felt it was time to get to know him better. When she flew back from Peru, she had a stop-off in Melbourne and told Alison of her decision to move there.

On this very same day, Alison found out her husband would not live more than a few more months. A brain tumour that had been dormant for years had suddenly returned. Soon Julie was dealing with both her own grief and the grief of her grandson and widowed daughter.

Julie felt as if her whole world had been stripped away. She had given up her job in Sydney; she had moved from Perth to Melbourne; and despite having a series of qualifications (two diplomas, a Master of Education, an MBA, a PhD in education and an almost-completed Master of Theology), her plans to go into full-time church ministry had not come to fruition either. In terms of classic stress indicators, Julie's dial was well and truly at maximum.

Yet Julie claims she is not desperate to go back to who she was five years ago. She explains that everything she has faced has made her the person she is today. She says she lacks nothing and feels quite rich, despite walking away from her business dramas with only a $50 cheque.

Julie puts much of this down to a coping strategy she learned 30 metres above the Amazonian jungle. When she and her friends moved on from Machu Picchu to an adventure walking across swinging bridges above the Amazon, Julie was way outside her comfort zone. Her friends seemed very confident, striding ahead. Julie was terrified, gripping the ropes on either side of the first bridge with white knuckles. The guide recognised she was on the verge of a panic attack, and he came back and stood one metre in front of her. He looked her in the eye and said, "There are eight more bridges, and you cannot go back! Just look at me and walk." She gripped his arms and started to inch forward across the bridge.

As she stayed glued to her guide, still trembling with fear, Julie was suddenly overcome by a truth that has sustained her every day since. She felt God was speaking to her: "This is exactly how I want you to live your life, Julie – looking at me always, and not looking down into the jungle or back at where you have come from." Julie says that by the seventh bridge she was skipping, and by the eighth she ran across.

Her load had been lightened, and she felt that God was with her and ahead of her. She had certainly faced her fears and her grief head-on, and this was a strengthening experience.

Georgia

Sometimes the conflicts we face in our lives are less personal and more about business and ethics. Many years ago, Georgia worked as a management consultant in a boutique international company. She enjoyed her role greatly, and she was pleased when, after four years in the organisation, she was invited to join the national management team.

However, the company had some financial difficulties. There were offices in more than one Australian city, and whilst Georgia's branch was highly profitable, the interstate offices were losing money at an alarming rate. Georgia's responsibilities were confined to the Melbourne office, but she experienced the brunt of the crisis when her bosses decided to withhold paying her bonus entitlements until their cash flow improved.

> "...I have learned the secret of being content in any and every situation, whether well fed or hungry, whether living in plenty or in want."[46]
>
> *The Apostle Paul*

Georgia did not have the time or energy for any conflict or confrontation, and anyway, she was incredibly loyal to the business and willing to wait and support her directors in their decision. However, after more than a year with no bonuses being paid (although they were a non-negotiable part of her remuneration package), she began to have cash flow issues herself. She approached her bosses to suggest it was time for the outstanding bonuses to be paid. Unfortunately, it appeared her bosses were losing track of their legal obligations to their staff. They continued to refuse to pay the bonuses, and it later appeared they were also behind in paying the compulsory contributions to their staff superannuation funds.

Georgia had been trying to support her bosses for years, and she considered herself to be a "peacemaker". However, she was not in a very peaceful situation. One day it dawned on her that far from being a true peacemaker, she was actually being an "appeaser". She was facilitating the injustice her bosses had adopted as a cash-flow strategy. So she decided to confront them with their legal obligations, and she made it clear she would not remain silent. In effect, she decided to "take up arms" to facilitate a "true peace".

The final outcome was a compromise. Georgia resigned – no longer willing to support her bosses in their approach to management – and accepted a reduced calculation of her bonuses in return for immediate payment. But she was also older and wiser, recognising now that appeasement was not a solution to injustice at all. She felt better after speaking the truth rather than avoiding conflict. Coming to grips with the dilemma was far more soul enriching than burying her head in the sand. (There is more of Georgia's story in Chapter 15.)

స

Research suggests that burying our grief is not a healthy way of responding to pain in our lives (although it can be the easier option when we are time-poor). Brené Brown says that if we numb our pain, we will also numb our joy.[47]

I am not an advocate of the idea that terrible things can be rationalised into being positive because we grow stronger from them. Bad things happen, and they cannot be made less "bad" because finally some good comes after. I believe that the true core of suffering is that it does not make any sense. If we could make sense of it, it would not hurt as much.

Nonetheless, we can still be enriched and strengthened by facing our pain rather than ignoring it, and by confronting conflict rather than appeasing it. It sounds corny, but it is the gritty irritation within the oyster shell that produces the pearl. Our character is refined in situations of conflict and not when we are just cruising along.

Unlike the other time-poor casualties explored in this book, I am not suggesting we search out or try to make more room for adversity in our lives. However, none of us will escape adversity. It can come when we least expect it. Any subsequent soul enrichment comes from our response to adversity and not from its wounds. However, there is potentially also soul enrichment to be found in embracing a different type of adversity – the adventure that might be found in pursuing a new job or embarking on a quest outside our comfort zone. When the odds are against us, there can be great joy in prevailing.

60 Second Solutions to Re-engage with Adversity

1. Recall Significant Incidents:
- From your childhood, what moment of stress or pain has made you stronger today? Ponder if there is a lesson to be appreciated.
- From your current circumstances, identify what is currently causing you the most conflict, and consider what you can learn from it.

2. Review Your Workplace:
- Recognise situations where you should not back down – for instance, if you identify bullying or injustice.
- Ask your colleagues to suggest what you can learn from a difficult situation.

3. Resolve for the Future:
- Decide that no matter what adversity you face, you will not lose faith in the things that really matter.
- Identify your closest allies, those you can rely on when stuff happens.
- Decide to embark on a short adventure in the next year to hone your survival skills.
- Decide to put aside one or two days in the next 12 months to go on a retreat for rejuvenation.

- Resolve to tackle an overwhelming task by breaking it into bite-sized pieces.

4. *Research and Imagine:*
   Search the internet for information on:
   - how to cope with suffering
   - the Holmes and Rahe Stress Scale
   - conflict-resolution skills
   - best short-break adventure holidays
   - tall-ship sailing trips
   - best holiday destinations for rest and retreat.

5. *Record in Your Notebook or on Your Electronic Device:*
   - Write a log of things you have learnt from difficult situations in your life.
   - Record the date you will go on a retreat to renew your strength.
   - Record a list of people who might like to share a short adventure with you.
   - Record an uplifting quote in your phone or notebook so you see it daily (for example, "The difference between stumbling blocks and stepping stones is how you use them"; or "Those who hope in the Lord will renew their strength – they will soar on wings like eagles"; or "Every moment is a fresh beginning.")

6. *Reach Out to Others:*
   - Contact someone with whom you are at loggerheads, and suggest it is time to find common ground or have a coffee together.
   - Contact a friend or counsellor whom you trust, and propose a time to brainstorm how to deal with the conflicts you are facing.
   - Contact a friend to suggest you enjoy an adventure together.
   - When someone is trying to pick a fight with you, don't bite back; rather ask how the issue can be resolved in a way which keeps you both happy.

7. *Refocus with a Time-Poor Prayer:*
   • Thank you God that you are bigger than everything tragic that happens in the world. I know I can never see the end before the beginning, and I know I will never understand why bad things happen, but please give me courage to face everything that comes my way. Please help me learn from everything I face. Comfort my soul.

8. *Rest for 60 Seconds:*
   • Stop everything; think of something difficult you have faced that you are grateful for right now; and rest in the knowledge that comfort is nearby.

Lengthier Remedies

• Go on a retreat to gain some distance from your troubles and to gather strength for the future.
• Go on an adventure to activate your adrenalin.
• Go sailing for a couple of hours on a tall ship.
• Speak with a counsellor about the things which bother you most.
• Go trekking for a couple of hours through some bushland.
• Read *The Shack* by William P. Young (Windblown Media, 2007).

Re-engaging with Our Internal Selves

ONE OF THE FIRST THINGS TO GO when we are overwhelmed with work and daily responsibilities is the care of our own internal well-being. Being stretched to the limit can easily mean we neglect the pursuit of clarity or wisdom in our lives. And there is nothing like being time-poor to help us dispense with serenity. We can also abandon any priority on health and vitality, and avoid spirituality all together.

These four casualties of our time-poor condition – Clarity, Serenity, Vitality and Spirituality – can all assist our soul enrichment if we nurture them. Following are some strategies on how to make sure we look after our internal selves, and so be strengthened to contribute good things to others.

"He who gets wisdom loves his own soul;
He who keeps understanding will find good."[48]
King Solomon

"It seems an odd idea to my students that poetry, like all art, leads us
away from itself, back to the world in which we live. It furnishes the vision.
It shows with a sudden intense clarity what is already there."[49]
Helen Bevington

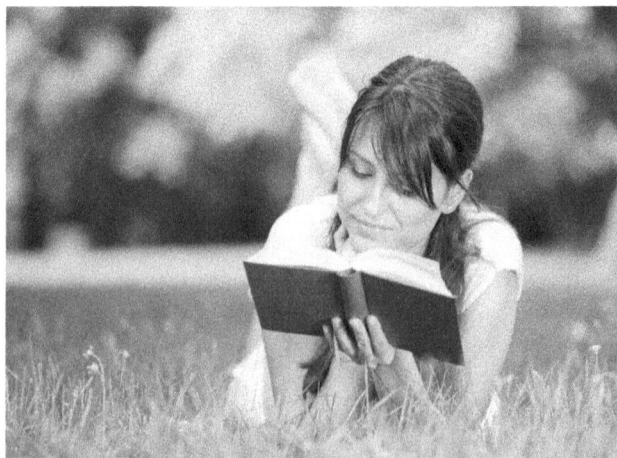

Chapter 10

❧

Clarity

How OFTEN DO WE HAVE clarity of mind when we are consumed by work and busyness? How can we best find wisdom when we are time-poor and living in survival mode? When my own soul has been in survival mode I have found my mind creeping into a state of fog. It is then all too easy to just keep following old familiar patterns in my daily decision-making and prioritising.

However, those default patterns do not always lead to the best outcomes. There is nothing like the return of clarity to bring back some enrichment to the soul.

Liang

When Liang married her husband, now an orthopaedic surgeon, she thought she had the perfect life. She was a corporate lawyer in a global investment bank in Sydney; she was living in a beautiful house on Sydney Harbour; and she had the perfect husband.

However, cracks began to show by about the third year of their marriage. Her "perfect husband" was not operating in the manner she most approved of, and she was trying hard to change him – particularly the way he studied for his medical exams. Liang had always been a very diligent student, and she could not understand how her husband could be studying "properly" in front of the television during commercial breaks. Further, her work at the investment bank was keeping her away until late each night, and her husband left for his work at the hospital by 6.00am each morning. They were hardly crossing paths.

To top it all off, Liang desperately wanted to have a baby but was not falling pregnant.

Liang was so busy with her work as a senior lawyer that she rarely had time to review or reflect on her life and choices. She was proud of her achievements and did not see anything wrong with her lifestyle. However, when two senior women, whom she greatly respected, separately challenged her by asking, "How long are you going to live like that?", she began to wonder if her life was in fact on the right path. Liang started in a new direction, seeing things more clearly when she made some changes.

Then there was a death in the family and Liang started to question what mattered most in life. She was thinking about death and the meaning of life in a whole new way. She realised that although she was young and healthy, death would inevitably become a fact of her life and it was just a matter of time. Liang considered what kind of legacy she wanted to leave behind for those who knew her.

> "The next best thing to being wise oneself is to live in a circle of those who are..."[50]
>
> *C.S. Lewis*

Although working on high-profile multi-billion dollar transactions had previously seemed like an important and proud achievement, suddenly it seemed immaterial and insignificant in the context of life, death and eternity. Liang concluded that being loved by God, loving God in return, and reflecting God's love by loving others were the most important things in life – things that had eternally lasting value.

Another of Liang's new directions was to adopt a mentor. She started to meet monthly with one of those two senior women. Before long she was questioning her obsession with prestige, career success and the money she was earning. Her mentor encouraged her to refocus on her relationship with God. Liang purchased a copy of a small book of daily Bible reflections and read this on the train each morning. She also changed the way she talked to God. Until then, she had her ten-year plan and went to God for his stamp of approval. Now she was consciously trying to get closer to God and find out what he wanted for her life.

Liang used other techniques to learn more about God in the context of her extremely busy work life. One was to buy a pocket-sized packet of cards with Bible verses written on them. Whenever she had a moment – walking between meetings, on the train or between cerebral tasks – she would pull out a card and quickly meditate on the text. She also tried to memorise the words for even quicker recall later. As well she printed the lyrics of her favourite gospel songs on small pieces of paper and kept them in her pocket diary. As with the Bible verses she memorised the song lyrics, and she would sing these songs whenever she had spare time, especially while walking.

Liang's mentor was a good sounding board and she helped Liang challenge some of her deeply held views. For the first time in her career, Liang considered whether she should go part-time, particularly because she was still having difficulty getting pregnant. For Liang, being in full-time work was exhausting (her work days often ended near midnight and she frequently worked on weekends). However, her supervising director at the investment bank convinced her that going part-time would be an unwise decision. This director pointed out that if she stayed on her current career path, her salary would significantly increase, and it would be a much easier and faster road to the top – but if she went part-time, neither of these goals could be guaranteed.

Liang tried to forget about the idea – she felt she did not have a good enough excuse to request a change to her role (especially since she didn't have the justification of children at home), and she thought she would be laughed at if she even suggested going part-time. Yet the inner desire to slow down did not go away.

Then Liang's decision was taken out of her hands. Unexpectedly, doctors found a lump in her stomach that they suspected was a tumour.

Given that she was being told the results might take a month before being available, Liang immediately asked her manager if she could go part-time whilst she was waiting. Her request was approved within 24 hours.

Liang had previously thought about death vicariously through the death of others, but this time she was forced to think about the possibility of her own death. During that month of waiting, she pondered deeply about death, and life after death. She found that her initial shock eventually turned into peace as she learnt to trust in God in matters of both life and death.

Happily, Liang only had a cyst and not a tumour in her stomach. But having been granted a part-time role, she stayed on in this arrangement. Within six months she was pregnant. Liang now has two beautiful little boys, and continues to work part-time in a global investment bank.

For Liang, clarity only came when she opened herself up to accountability with an older and wiser mentor, and when she focussed on her relationship with God in a new way.

Elizabeth

Elizabeth's role in procurement creates multiple strategic dilemmas, so she is always happy to seek wise counsel from colleagues and authors. She has also found it a challenge to keep a clear head for all of the non-work related areas of her life.

In order to make informed decisions, Elizabeth has adopted a full suite of mentors – one for each of the main areas of her life. She has a financial adviser, a legal mentor, a personal coach, a church counsellor, a health trainer and a business mentor. Elizabeth has created a diverse network where she can call on different experts as needed, and this has often given her confidence to move forward when otherwise she might have been uncertain.

> "The Eternal's directions are correct, giving satisfaction to the heart. God's commandments are clear, lending clarity to the eyes."[51]
>
> *King David*

Elizabeth also loves books, and she generally has a pile of them sitting by her bedside waiting to be finished. She tries to keep up the habit of reading a little before she goes to sleep each night. She also likes to pick up the Bible to look for wisdom, relying on the fact that it tells her that if she wants wisdom, she should ask God and it will be given to her.[52] And she has joined a local library to stop herself buying more and more books to fill her shelves at home. There is nothing like a library fine to encourage you to finish a book by a certain date.

✑

We now live in an information-rich age. Never before have we been able to access so much information with so little effort.

However, high volumes of information do not guarantee clarity. Remember that information is not necessarily knowledge; knowledge is not necessarily understanding; understanding is not necessarily wisdom; and insight might well be something else completely! A good starting point is to begin with human mentors – there is no shame in seeking out wise counsel from those whose experience we respect.

60 Second Solutions to Re-engage with Clarity

1. *Recall Significant Incidents:*
   - From your childhood, what is a piece of advice given to you which made a lasting difference? Ponder how you can continue to apply this advice.
   - From your current experience, where does your greatest clarity come from? Consider how to access this source more often.

2. *Review Your Workplace:*
   - Ask colleagues or managers for their best tips for your success.
   - Find moments when you can share a gem of wisdom.
   - Find someone who can answer an important question for you.
   - Read a few verses from the *Book of Proverbs* in the Bible.

3. *Resolve for the Future:*
   - Choose a wise counsellor whom you want to learn from.
   - Decide when you will commit to meeting with a mentor.
   - Choose a book you want to read which will add to your wisdom, understanding or clarity about life.
   - Decide to try a series of passwords that remind you of inspirational sayings or encouraging quotes (for example, using the first letter of each word in the phrase).
   - Plan that when you have to say no to someone, you will say it very clearly and without ambivalence – for example, "I've thought about that, and the answer is no. Definitely no."

4. *Research and Imagine:*
   Search the internet for information on:
   - quotes about wisdom
   - how to be wise
   - clear-thinking techniques.

5. *Record in Your Notebook or on Your Electronic Device:*
   - Write down the significant dreams you remember.
   - Record (or take snapshots of) an inspiring quote.
   - Record moments of insight as they occur to you.
   - List the books you would love to read.
   - Download an electronic version of a book.
   - Download an electronic version of the Bible.

6. *Reach Out to Others:*
   - Contact an "elder statesperson" whom you respect for their wisdom, and ask if you can meet to seek their advice about something.
   - Call someone who might be willing to act as a mentor to you.
   - Pause before making a decision, and call a trusted adviser to double check your thinking.

7. *Refocus with a Time-Poor Prayer:*
   - Thank you God that you are full of wisdom. And thank you that you have promised to give me wisdom if I ask. I am asking for wisdom! Please give me clarity of mind to know how to live and how better to understand the world around me. Teach my soul.

8. *Rest for 60 Seconds:*
   - Stop everything; think of some wise advice you are grateful for right now; and rest in the knowledge that if you ask God for wisdom then he will give it to you.

Lengthier Remedies

- Meet with a mentor regularly.
- Review and read your electronic books when travelling on public transport or pausing between meetings.
- Read for 15 minutes before going to sleep.
- Choose a book you haven't had time to read and listen to it as a "talking book" when driving in the car.
- Go for a walk and think about how you are living your life, and how it makes you feel.
- Read *The Purpose Driven Life – What on Earth Am I Here For?* by Rick Warren (Zondervan, 2002).

"But I do know focusing on the exterior doesn't make me happy. If I want peace and serenity, it won't be reached by getting thinner or fatter."[53]

Elle Macpherson

"God, give me grace to accept with serenity the things that cannot be changed, Courage to change the things which should be changed, and the Wisdom to distinguish the one from the other. Living one day at a time, Enjoying one moment at a time, Accepting hardship as a pathway to peace, Taking, as Jesus did, this sinful world as it is, Not as I would have it, Trusting that You will make all things right..."[54]

Reinhold Niebuhr

Chapter 11

ॐ

Serenity

I HAVE ALWAYS ADMIRED people who seem centred, serene and at peace – like the convent nuns who practise silence and contemplation. There is something reassuring about the fact that not everyone in the world is stressed-out, frantic and tethered to computers and mobile phones.

However, it is not easy to stay calm when ordinary troubles assail us. Many people struggled to make ends meet when the global financial crisis was in full swing, and some were sued or stolen from. Such day-to-day stresses can easily rob us of our time and our serenity.

Nalini

Nalini has only just discovered that she can be "calm" after 30 years of being an incorrigible workaholic. She was running her own public affairs and marketing business; she was bringing up two daughters; she was the main breadwinner as her husband was an artist; she was renovating a house; and she often found herself working at 3.00 or 4.00am in the morning.

Nalini describes her experience of being a workaholic as "always spinning out of control". She knew in her heart that this was unsustainable, but it was the death of her father that forced her to change. She could see how his expectations had forced her and her brother and sister to be workaholics – their main strategy for seeking his approval – and she did not want to have the same effect on her own children.

Nalini took some drastic action. She was at that time working in the corporate sector, and she sought and won funding to get herself a coach. She also found a Roman Catholic establishment where she committed herself to a four-day silent retreat. Yes, that's correct – no talking at all. Apparently the nuns would gather the women attending each afternoon and talk them through a contemplative topic, but no one was allowed to speak in return. This was a radical way to force reflection.

It was during this retreat that Nalini came across the proverb that counsels: "Do not wear yourself out to get rich; have the wisdom to show restraint."[55] This seemed like a direct reminder to her that the workaholic lifestyle was not good for the soul.

Nalini then found another consultant who was able to assess her emotional intelligence. This test clearly showed she was very low on the "calm meter". She was able to identify the core planks of her workaholism, and so she began the process of dismantling the whole habit.

> "Despair is the damp of hell; rejoicing is the serenity of heaven."[56]
>
> *John Donne*

Nalini created four core techniques to facilitate a change in her approach to work. She commenced her days with a prayer-time with God; followed by iPhone alerts to read significant Bible verses during the day; followed by filling in a gratitude journal each night. And her fourth technique was to watch her physical reactions to things. When the familiar tightness in her chest started (usually associated with a stressful situation she felt she had to resolve), she would stand up and shake out her arms, breathe deeply three times and force herself to let go of the stress.

Nalini had felt stress and worry all of her life. Now she was trying to draw on a calm place. Part of her strategy was to take four weeks of annual leave in a row – something she had not done for 25 years.

Another strategy she used to break the dominance of work was to travel into the city to meet with people, instead of just staying tied to her suburban office and desk.

An interesting outcome of these new techniques is that after being re-assessed by her emotional intelligence consultant, Nalini now has "calmness" as a core strength rather than an absent quality. A further outcome is that she will take five minutes to stay still and reflect before a meeting, and she sees this as "a valid use of time" – something she would never have considered in the past. She has always had a remedial massage once a month; however, her masseur has recently confirmed that her muscles have become far more relaxed. Also, whenever possible, Nalini now travels by public transport and listens to contemplative music as another way of ensuring she brings some calm into her busy schedule.

Nalini has adopted these conscious, intentional behaviours to change her whole approach to life, her work and her serenity.

Lynette

Lynette is the head of the middle school at a private school, and she claims she is stronger and calmer because of her habit of rising every day before 6.00am to walk for half an hour beside the nearby beach. She says she always thinks of God as she sees the sunrise and watches the lapping water. She finds this daily walk very peaceful and soothing, and she says it helps her to start her day in a centred frame of mind.

Anne

I recently had a disturbing experience which brought home how important it is to fiercely guard our serenity.

The night before my 50th birthday it was evident my husband needed to get to hospital quickly. He had developed a hernia which was causing him excruciating pain. I got up early on the morning of my birthday, called his doctor, picked up a referral and took my husband to the emergency section of a local hospital.

I worked from home that afternoon and then visited him that night. I found he had had a terrible allergic reaction (apparently a one in 40,000 chance) to the fluid given to him before a CT scan. His eyes were all puffy, he could barely speak and he had only survived the episode because of the steroids and other drugs that had been immediately pumped into his body. Yet I drove toward home content because although he looked terrible, he was alive! In fact, despite the fact he had forgotten my birthday (which is very unusual for my husband, who is a prolific gift giver) I had been happy and serene all day long.

That is, until I couldn't find a take-away chicken shop.

I did not feel like cooking dinner when I left the hospital around 9.30pm, so instead of going straight home, I headed off in search of food. It was only after driving for more than a quarter of an hour that I was suddenly overwhelmed with self-pity. It was my 50th birthday; my husband was in hospital; we hadn't had our romantic birthday dinner (in fact, he had forgotten all about my birthday); I was all alone; and most tragically, *I couldn't find a take-away chicken shop!*

The feeling of despair which swamped me was so unfamiliar that it really took me by surprise. I had been happy and content all day until that point, and I had been enjoying my serenity. I made an immediate decision to just ignore the whole self-pity feeling. I wanted my serenity back, and I couldn't see the point of descending into gloom. And then I found a chicken shop – so all was right with the world!

This event reinforced my view that when our serenity is challenged, we can sometimes hang on to it until a "last straw" threatens us, but it is still possible to return to calmness and serenity. There is an element of personal choice involved in maintaining our peaceful state of mind and heart, despite the disturbances of life.

ॐ

My perspective on inner peace has definitely been influenced by a conversation I had with my father when I was a teenager. He told me that if I was feeling sick in my stomach with worry (which I was at the time), then I was not trusting God. He then encouraged me to pray because God is bigger than anything we have to face, and he is able to help us.

> "Come to me, all you who are weary and burdened, and I will give you rest...for I am gentle and humble in heart, and you will find rest for your souls."[57]
>
> *Jesus*

Somehow this advice has stuck with me throughout my life, and in truth, I actually find it hard to worry about anything for long! I figure that if things go belly-up, then there will always be another adventure on the horizon. Life is too short to be anxious about things we cannot change. So it is worth holding on to things loosely, and not letting the noise of life distract us from the peace and calm that can come when we look beyond the rat race.

There is also good sense in inviting other more qualified people to intervene and assess our situation. And of course, identifying a location which facilitates our peace can also increase our serenity of soul.

60 Second Solutions to Re-engage with Serenity

1. Recall Significant Incidents:
- From your childhood, what occasion led to one of your most peaceful moments? Consider how to connect again with that moment.
- From your current experience, what is the location where you feel the greatest serenity? Ponder how you can visit that spot more often.

2. Review Your Workplace:
- Recognise colleagues who exude calm and ask them how they do it.
- Find opportunities to minimise the stress that those around you experience.

- Make a cup of tea or coffee, a hot chocolate or a warm blackcurrant drink when a quick refreshment will help.
- Do one thing that calms you while drinking your warm beverage – such as sketching a picture or some new house plans, gazing at a beautiful view or watering the nearby pot-plants.
- Find a moment to stop, take a deep breath, then expel all the air to remove as much carbon dioxide from your system as possible.
- Refuse to think about work for one minute while you look out of the window or at a beautiful picture.
- Play a recording of your favourite calming music.
- Suggest to your management that they hire an in-house neck masseur to work on the staff once a month.

3. *Resolve for the Future:*
   - Decide what you will say no to in the coming year (and consider that when you say yes to something, it usually means you have to say no in another area of your life).
   - Decide what you will read, who you will speak to, what you will do and how you will think to facilitate your serenity.
   - Decide when in the next 12 months you will have one or two days to go on a retreat.
   - Decide to find an exercise routine that involves disciplined stretching and breathing.
   - Decide to focus on something else, rather than the thing that is worrying you, when your stomach starts to churn with anxiety.

4. *Research and Imagine:*
   - Find a YouTube recording of a calming piece of music.
   - Find images of the most peaceful places on earth.
   Search the internet for information on:
   - stress management
   - the location of retreats in your area
   - therapeutic masseurs who do home visits in your area.

5. *Record in Your Notebook or on Your Electronic Device:*
   - Write a list of the things which are crowding your mind or worrying you, and schedule a time to deal with them in the future.
   - Make a list of your preferred "trusted advisers" in various areas (legal, financial, spiritual etc.) and schedule a time to contact them in the future.
   - Make a list of the books you will take on retreat in the next 12 months.

6. *Reach Out to Others:*
   - Don't contact anyone for 24 hours, but instead reflect on your key priorities for the coming year and write yourself a list. Only then contact a friend to tell them what you have decided.
   - Contact a friend and arrange a time to discuss strategies for finding peace.
   - When someone tries to get under your skin or push your buttons, smile questioningly and say, "Really?"
   - Ask a friend who knows you well how they think you are faring in the serenity space.

7. *Refocus with a Time-Poor Prayer:*
   - Thank you God that you are in control and that you bring peace and calm in a storm. Thank you that you bring comfort where there is stress. Please help me not to fear, and help me learn to trust in your help. I'd love to be more at peace. Warm my soul.

8. *Rest for 60 Seconds:*
   - Stop everything; think of something that calms your soul that you are grateful for right now; breathe deeply, and rest in the knowledge that it is possible to be content whether you are thriving and prosperous or not.

Lengthier Remedies

- Go to the peaceful spot in your workplace or near your home and regather your strength.
- Have a massage or a therapeutic pampering session.
- Attend a retreat for one or two days where you spend time in prayer and contemplation of your priorities for the coming year.
- Spend an hour fishing off a jetty.
- Spend an hour identifying stars through a telescope.
- Try some gentle exercise that helps you stop and breathe and be.
- Read *Little Book of Calm* by Paul Wilson (Penguin Books, 1996).

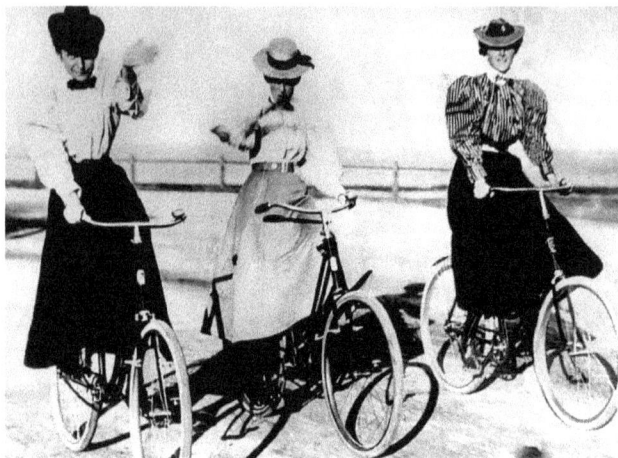

"There is a vitality, a life force, an energy, a quickening that is translated through you into action, and because there is only one of you in all of time, this expression is unique. And if you block it, it will never exist through any other medium and it will be lost."[58]
Martha Graham

"I draw a boundary around my exercise time and protect it like a mamma bear protects her cubs. But there's a more important reason why I protect my exercise time and that's because it's as good for my spirit as it is for my body. I'm more likely to be at the top of my game mentally and emotionally when I exercise; I think more clearly and find that I'm more creative."[59]
Diane Paddison

Chapter 12

ॐ

Vitality

IT IS VERY EASY TO NEGLECT health, exercise, activity and vitality when life is busy and all-consuming. However, for some it is actually making that bit of space to be involved in a physical activity that keeps them sane. Following a couple of failed attempts to attend a gym after buying a membership, I invested in a "home gym" which can be used without wasting any more money (or any extra time travelling). My other main form of exercise is jogging to the train in the morning (I'd like to say this is because I am conscious of fitness, but the truth is that I am often running late!), and I usually make the effort to walk up the escalators rather than standing still for any journey. Far from exercise taking up time, these last two techniques actually add to my fitness while saving time!

Gayle

Gayle has always loved horse riding. She grew up with horses on a few acres of farm land, and she finds it enormously enriching to leave the city limits and drink in the peace and beauty of the countryside. There is nothing more joyful for her than to saddle up a horse and ride across that countryside with the wind in her face.

Accordingly, Gayle tried to convince her oldest daughter, Hilary, that "pony club" was a great idea for the weekends. Unfortunately for Gayle, Hilary wasn't at all interested in riding. Luckily, her second daughter, Nina, loved horses, and so the tradition of a ride on the weekend was forged.

However, finding time for a few hours in the countryside each week has not been easy. Gayle's life is complicated.

She has been stretched for time ever since she first married. Being a radiologist was already a demanding profession, but marrying a man who was training to be a minister in the church certainly added to the pressures. Soon she and her husband were blessed with three beautiful children. Gayle had not planned to be a minister's wife, but once she made the decision, she loved it and threw herself into the work of the church. She ran a Bible study, organised groups for mothers with babies, ran praise and worship services, facilitated women's camps and retreats, and organised groups which taught kids how to pray. She also continued to work as a radiologist three days a week, and she was eventually appointed head of the medical imaging department at a prestigious tertiary hospital.

Gayle's life was already short of discretionary time with all these responsibilities when some shocking news completely changed the direction of her family. Gayle's son was found to be suffering from a degenerative muscle disease. By the time he was 11 years old Daniel was already confined to a wheelchair. It became even more important for Gayle to have paid work for at least three days every week. In addition to the motorised wheelchair, they needed a disabled person's bathroom, ramps instead of stairs and a van to transport the wheelchair along with the family.

Gayle has thought a lot about what will give joy to her son. Given that his physical activity has now been severely curtailed, she has brought some vitality into his world by bringing home a puppy. Outings to puppy training school and the ongoing companionship of a small furry friend have certainly brought enrichment to Daniel's soul.

I can personally testify to the joy that a "little white dog" has brought to my home. I always point to my pup Billy and explain to others, "This is what happens when you are in your 40s and you don't have children – you get one of these!" Billy brings a huge amount of laughter to me and my husband, and if nothing else, he forces us to go for that walk we might otherwise avoid through tiredness, busyness or laziness.

> "Trust and reverence the Lord, and turn your back on evil; when you do that, then you will be given renewed health and vitality."[60]
>
> *King Solomon*

Gayle's life is not as sociable, or as neat and tidy, as many others. Gayle and her husband rarely go out to dinner or have others over for a meal. They already have a vast number of human interactions in various church activities. Gayle does try, however, to get to the gym at least once a week as she says this gives her more energy for everything else.

There is also one social activity that Gayle does indulge in: she has formed the tradition of regularly taking an hour to "go out for coffee" with her daughter Hilary. Whilst this is not strictly a physical activity, it is still getting out of the house and having quality time with one of her children. And then there is horse riding with Nina.

In order to take those few hours on the weekend, Gayle has had to let go of other pressing things. Her garden always has more weeds than she would like, and her house is more untidy than her husband would like. But when forming her priorities, Gayle has reached the firm conclusion that she would rather have weeds and dust (or pay for a gardener and a cleaner) than miss out on time with her children, her husband, her horse, her countryside and her God. These are the things that enrich Gayle's soul.

Ilana

Unlike Gayle, Ilana, a sanitation specialist, had been passively "anti-sport" and "anti-exercise" for nearly 40 years (and perhaps just a little lazy when it came to physical activity!). However, she was suddenly forced to consider finding time in her life for fitness when she was diagnosed with high blood pressure. Ilana was given two choices: medication for the rest of her life or starting an exercise regime.

There is nothing like a medical crisis to help you find space in your life to focus more on healthy living. So Ilana found a gym near her home and dedicated 50 minutes, three nights a week, to an exercise program.

The thing that surprised Ilana was how much better she felt in her mind and body. She describes it as a "wonderful change" in which she feels more active, less achy and stiff, and even less cold. And using classic "soul-rich" strategies, Ilana used the gym to satisfy other parts of her needy soul. She used the available television screen to catch up on current affairs, and she allowed herself to enjoy the solitude of the experience (earplugs inserted and all outside contact avoided), which for an introvert is a blissful experience. (There is more about Ilana in Chapter 14.)

Bonnie

Bonnie is a school teacher who works over 60 hours every week, handling her preparation, her classes, her marking, her report writing and all the after-hours meetings and student activities. For years she kept her soul alive through physical activity and vitality. She would go dancing three nights a week, she loved bushwalking and she always tried to find time to exercise at the gym.

Then Bonnie experienced a disaster. She had a sporting injury and hurt one of her legs – and this brought an end to all of her physical activities. She felt like the part of her life which had given her the most joy had been snatched away.

Bonnie had to search for new ways to bring some joy to her soul. In fact, this was the point in Bonnie's life when she learnt to be still, and to enjoy what she was able to do (instead of grieving over what she could not do). She started to re-engage with her friends on a more intimate basis, and when her leg began to heal, she learnt to enjoy a ten-minute walk instead of a long bushwalk.

Bonnie's leg is much stronger now, but she has adopted a much wider range of strategies to keep her soul enriched.

൙

Vitality is more than just exercising our bodies. Physical strength is helpful to live life fully, but our bodies *will* grow old. Mental acuity can remain even when the body is broken, so it is important to also exercise our minds.

But there is a vitality that is deeper than both of these things – it is a strength of spirit in the face of life's storms. Alice Walker, an American author well known for her novel *The Colour Purple*, has written a moving account of horrors from Rwanda, Eastern Congo and Palestine. At one point she visits Gaza City and describes the grief of a group of women who have all lost children, husbands and friends in military bombardments. What happens next takes her by surprise. The women lead her to a room with loud music playing and they all begin to dance. Alice writes:

> "If you lose hope, somehow you lose that vitality that keeps life moving, you lose that courage to be, that quality that helps you to go on in spite of all."[61]
>
> *Martin Luther King, Jr*

> ...the rising that always comes from such dancing; the sense of joy, unity, solidarity, and gratitude to be in the best place one could be on earth, with sisters who have experienced the full measure of disaster and have the heart to rise above it. The feeling of love was immense... this Spirit that knows how to dance in the face of disaster, will never be crushed.[62]

The soul enrichment that comes from this dancing has lots of layers. In this account there is a social connection, a creative outlet, a refusal to accept injustice, a spiritual experience, an atmosphere of love and a vitality that prevails over great hardship.

60 Second Solutions to Re-engage with Vitality

1. *Recall Significant Incidents:*
   - From your childhood, what physical activity sticks in your mind that gave you great joy? Ponder how to replicate the joy in your current circumstances.
   - From your current experience, what activity makes you feel the most energised? Consider how to maximise the chances of engaging in this activity.

2. *Review Your Workplace:*
   - Find physical obstacles that can be used for exercise (for instance, walk up the stairs instead of taking the elevator).
   - Find opportunities to do neck and arm exercises at your desk.
   - Brainstorm with a colleague about best health strategies.
   - Sneak opportunities to play some great music and dance a jig around your office.
   - Suggest that your organisation enters a team in a fun run or basketball competition.
   - Walk to your colleagues to speak with them, rather than sending emails.
   - Consider going for a walk instead of making a cup of coffee.

3. *Resolve for the Future:*
   - Decide to take a multivitamin tablet each day.
   - Decide to keep a stash of energy snacks handy.
   - Decide to do a series of stretches each morning as you rise from bed.
   - Decide to join an association which facilitates your favourite activity.
   - Decide to put aside some time in the future to walk, swim, bike ride, jog, climb, dance or whatever else you choose, and put it into the diary.
   - Plan a holiday that involves lots of physical exercise.

- Decide that when you pass a set of stairs, you will skip up and down a few stairs before continuing on your way.

4. *Research and Imagine:*
   Search the internet for information on:
   - exercises to do at your desk
   - the best multivitamin tablet
   - local sports teams (such as basketball, netball, hockey, soccer, tennis, squash, swimming, athletics)
   - local organisations or clubs that facilitate your favourite sport or other activity (such as horse riding, rock climbing, bushwalking, dancing, bike riding, fencing, roller skating, ice skating)
   - local boot camps or personal trainers.

5. *Record in Your Notebook or on Your Electronic Device:*
   - Write a list of the quick exercises and stretches you hope to do each day.
   - Record the date you plan to visit a personal trainer, and make a list of friends who might consider going with you.

6. *Reach Out to Others:*
   - Contact a friend who enjoys similar physical activities to you, and suggest you catch up to undertake an activity together.
   - Contact a medical professional for a health audit on your body, including any areas where you need to be proactive.

7. *Refocus with a Time-Poor Prayer:*
   - Thank you God that you are always working, but you also know how to rest. Please help me to be as healthy and as active as possible, and please remind me to make good choices and give me the strength to follow through. Enliven my soul.

8. *Rest for 60 Seconds:*
   - Stop everything; think of some activity you are grateful for right now; and rest in the knowledge that activity and recreation are restorative.

Lengthier Remedies

- Take five minutes to do some exercises and stretches in the office.
- Go for a bike ride.
- Go for a walk with a friend, or walk a dog.
- Buy a piece of home-gym equipment.
- Use that piece of home-gym equipment.
- Go on a short camping trip overnight.
- Learn to dance.
- Read *The Women's Health Big Book of 15-Minute Workouts: A Leaner, Sexier, Healthier You – In 15 Minutes a Day!* by Selene Yeager (Rodale, 2011).

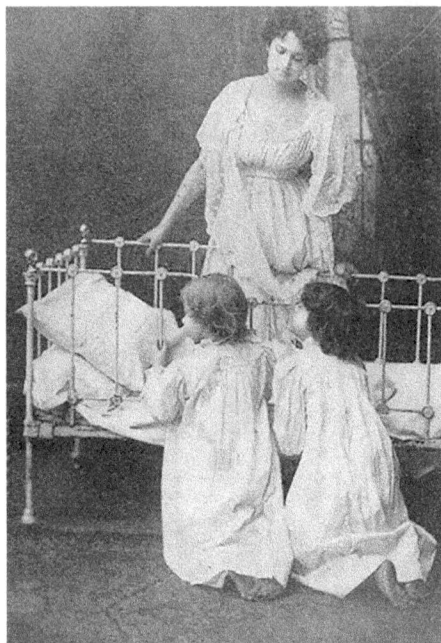

"Biblical truth and spirituality is not a relationship to the *word* god, or to the *idea* god. It is a relationship to the one who is there, which is an entirely different concept."[63]
Francis Schaeffer

"There are many in the world who are dying for a piece of bread but there are many more dying for a little love. The poverty in the West is a different kind of poverty – it is not only a poverty of loneliness but also of spirituality. There's a hunger for love, as there is a hunger for God."[64]
Mother Teresa

Chapter 13

౭

Spirituality

IT IS OFTEN SAID THAT WE NEED to attend to mind, body and spirit. But it is very easy to neglect the spiritual side to the world given that it is arguably the most controversial arena. Is there life after death? Are there good and evil spirits in the world? Is there a god who hears our prayers? Did Jesus come into the world to bring forgiveness and restoration to a fallen human race? Millions of people throughout the ages have answered yes to such questions. In fact, the 20th century's brief experiment with a "godless" communist state did not prevail, with faith in God springing up all over modern Russia and China.

One encouraging thing to remember, when work and time constraints restrict us from engaging with many of the other time-poor casualties described in these pages, is that there will always be capacity for a spiritual life. This is particularly true if we focus on the implications of God being present with us (rather than us doing duties for God).

I am not suggesting that being "spiritual" is only related to the supernatural. In fact, *many* of the time-poor casualties described in this book have spiritual elements to them, including the way we make loving choices in our lives and the way we appreciate the beautiful world around us. However, the spirituality focus of this chapter is about personal transformation that comes from an encounter with a god that is not of our own making.

Stephanie

Stephanie was not one to neglect the spiritual pursuits in life, despite being a highly successful professional woman. For years she was a self-professed workaholic, mostly working in corporate risk within the highly male-oriented engineering and construction sector. Despite her challenging career, however, Steph spent more than 20 years exploring every spiritual path that offered some form of guidance and inner peace – every path except Christianity that is. Until she was 40, Steph rejected Christianity as a materialistic and patriarchal religion that could not provide her with spiritual answers. However, she always believed there was "something out there" – something that was bigger than her and able to guide her.

Her mother had been a big fan of astrology and tarot cards, and Steph was familiar with having her fortune told as a child. She kept up her mother's interest in horoscopes, tarot cards, numerology and praying to ancient Greek and Roman gods, and also explored runestones, chakras, energy signatures, colour auras, white magic, feng shui, crystals, vibrations, reflexology, reincarnation, Taoism and Buddhism. Eventually she found a form of Hindu meditation that she practised three times a week, rising at 4.00am each day to attend the studio.

Steph was seeking peace – but she always had a very busy brain. Despite keeping up her spiritual journey, she did not find the soul enrichment she was hoping for. Each time she explored a particular path, she eventually found something that displeased her and moved on to the next spiritual offering. Nothing seemed to calm her soul.

It was after becoming more and more exhausted by work, her failed marriage and her unsatisfactory spiritual quest that Steph decided to go on a "girls' holiday" to Spain. Even when her three friends pulled out of the trip, Steph forged ahead. It was a disaster. Rather than having a fun restorative holiday where she could recharge her batteries, Steph found herself on a tour with a bunch of "oldies" and came home more exhausted than when she left. However, the trip reinforced one key belief. Steph was definitely not interested in the religion she saw parading through the Spanish streets at Easter time, with its silver and gold statues and exorbitant pomp and ceremony. She knew very little about Christianity, but she did have some vague idea that the main guy, Jesus Christ, had been relatively humble, and had ridden on a donkey.

> "The Lord is my shepherd, I shall not want. He makes me lie down in green pastures. He leads me beside still waters. He restores my soul..."[65]
>
> *King David*

Soon after getting back to Australia, Steph contracted a debilitating bout of flu and ended up in bed struggling to recover. She was at her wit's end and did an uncharacteristic thing. In desperation she called out to an unknown God, and suggested that if that God was there, she would really like a sign. Within a few days she was unexpectedly made redundant, and within weeks she found herself regularly visiting a house church where she had been invited by some people from work.

What she found there seemed far removed from the patriarchal, materialistic religiosity she had observed in Spain. So when her friends invited her to adopt Jesus as her personal saviour, she thought she would give it a go. She had tried every other spiritual offering that had presented itself, so she couldn't see any difference in giving this Jesus a whirl. She could always move on again if it did not deliver a result, just as she had with the various other New Age pursuits of her past.

What Steph did not expect was the immediate encounter with God that occurred when she prayed with her friends. She says that as they all prayed she became "awash with God's Spirit". She was not expecting the experience to last, although she did consider it a pretty cool start to this new experiment with Christianity. To her surprise, she experienced a kind of spiritual euphoria that continued for a number of weeks.

That was around eight years ago, and Steph says that now her search is over. She says that none of her earlier spiritual pursuits came close to providing her with the inner peace, guidance and loving grace she has found from connecting with Jesus. She also found, after a lot of prayer in those early months, that she experienced a freedom and release from many of the negative after-effects of some of her previous spiritual connections.

Another thing Steph had not expected was the negative reaction from her friends to her newfound faith. They had tolerated her exploration of different spiritual directions (some relatively mainstream, others quite alternative), but when Steph became a Christian, suddenly she was uncool. For the first time in her life her friends accused her of being a spiritual loony.

She was intrigued to think that praying to ancient Roman gods was OK by her friends while forging a relationship with Jesus was not considered acceptable. But she did not mind. She had found a spiritual answer that had evaded her for the first four decades of her life.

Gayle

Chapter 12 recounts the story of Gayle, the radiologist married to a church minister. As if trying to juggle her professional work and the care of her husband and three children was not a feat in itself, Gayle also juggles her multiple church activities, the disability of her son and the care of her two daughters in the context of her son's escalating needs. This is a woman with a lot on her plate.

I have spoken at length with Gayle to find out how she stays sane, where she finds her joy and basically "how she does it". It is clear that everything for Gayle begins with her relationship with God. She claims that without daily prayer and Bible reading, she does not feel the same presence of God and his strength and guidance each day.

She also takes every opportunity to be thankful, and to get away on her own for around an hour a day (when possible) to spend more quality time with God.

Rana

Chapter 7 describes Rana's journey from working in a homeless shelter with her husband and two small children to her new profession as a lawyer. However, she did not travel an easy road. Not long into her work at the shelter, Rana moved into a "survival mode" season when she unexpectedly became an unsupported single mother. Survival mode meant that she simply focussed on what had to be done each day to get through this difficult time.

Eventually Rana realised she had completely neglected her spiritual well-being, and she had "nothing left in the tank" to sustain her. She then found a Roman Catholic Church retreat which she attended. She explained to the priest that she did not have the time to pray, but he did not let her get away with this conclusion. Instead he taught her to pray in the context of where she was each day.

Rather than feeling she needed to set aside time to pray, she could *find* God in whatever task she was doing. The result for Rana was that she felt reconnected to God and her serenity returned. After "running on empty" for years, she regained an inner peace that began to heal her broken heart.

> "...to be spiritually minded is life and peace."[66]
>
> *The Apostle Paul*

Rana also loved to sing, but because her local community choir met on a night when she had other responsibilities, a number of years went by when she did not sing with the choir. However, when she was finally able to join, Rana found great joy each time she participated. She particularly loves the gospel-style songs – singing about rivers, peace and journeys through life is for her a very uplifting experience. She says that everyone who comes to sing with the choir seems to let go of their personal burdens as the music begins. Rana finds music to be life giving.

When I was young, I read the story of an exceedingly time-poor woman, Susanna Wesley (mother to John and Charles Wesley, leaders in the 18th-century Methodist movement). Her husband was a busy preacher; she gave birth to 19 children (only ten of which survived infancy); one of her children was disabled; and Susanna herself was often sick. She grew food for the family, taught lessons to her children and ran the busy household almost singlehandedly. Yet even in the midst of this hectic schedule, Susanna was determined to spend time praying. She had no quiet place to go, so she made a rule with the children that when she put her apron over her head at the kitchen table, they were not allowed to disturb her as she was talking to God. Susanna's example shows us that no matter how chaotic our day is, there is always the possibility of taking a moment to pray.

Listening to inspiring music (or making that music yourself) can also open the door to spiritual enrichment. The wonderful thing about music is that it can create a calming backdrop to an otherwise chaotic day.

60 Second Solutions to Re-engage with Spirituality

1. *Recall Significant Incidents:*
   - From your childhood, recall a time when you felt close to God and ponder how that came about.
   - From your current experience, recall an occasion when a prayer was answered, and consider asking God for more help more often.

2. *Review Your Workplace:*
   - Pray for your colleagues and business to thrive.
   - When times get tough, ask God for help.
   - Take a moment to read a prayer from the *Book of Psalms* in the Bible.
   - Look out of a window towards the horizon and consider how big the world is and how minuscule we are in comparison.

3. *Resolve for the Future:*
   - Decide that you will look at your food before beginning to eat, give thanks for the meal, and appreciate the colours, texture and smell of the food.
   - Decide that when you are in doubt about how to proceed, you will ask God for guidance.

4. *Research and Imagine:*
   - Consider how you will feel if you discover your days are numbered – has your life been full of what matters, or do you need to change something?

   Search the internet for information on:
   - how do I know if God exists?
   - who was Jesus?
   - what is meant by the grace of God?
   - how do I learn to pray?
   - what is Business Alpha?

5. *Record in Your Notebook or on Your Electronic Device:*
   - Write a list of biblical and poetical quotes that inspire you.
   - Record the things you have learned about God, eternity and grace.

6. *Reach Out to Others:*
   - Contact someone whose faith you respect, and suggest to them it is time to catch up to chat.
   - Contact someone who you know is a prayerful person, and ask them to pray for you.
   - Offer to pray for someone who is in need.
   - Contact someone who knows a good church, and ask them about it.

7. *Refocus with a Time-Poor Prayer:*
   - Thank you God for being there. Thank you that it's not all up to me. Thank you that you sent Jesus to save us from judgment and death. Help me know what it means that you let your own son die for

me. Please help me to be free of all the things that could possibly enslave me. Please remind me to ask you for help. Please give me a new spiritual awakening. Teach me to pray. Fill my soul.

8. *Rest for 60 Seconds:*
   - Stop everything; think of something about God that you are grateful for right now; and rest in the knowledge that God is bigger than us, personally interested in us and able to open up a wider vista to us.

Lengthier Remedies

- Attend a Business Alpha class.
- Attend a church service or a group to look at the Bible.
- Join a book club and study a spiritual book.
- Meet a couple of friends to support one another and pray for one another.
- Read *Spiritual Disciplines Handbook: Practices That Transform Us* by Adele Ahlberg Calhoun (IVP Books, 2005).

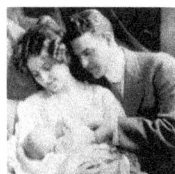

Re-engaging with Our External Expression

THE THINGS WE WANT to express from our hearts and minds can sometimes be strangled because of the busyness of life. Being time-poor can almost guarantee we neglect being creative. There is also a possibility we will struggle with honesty and integrity, suppress our good humour and lose sight of the centrality of love.

These final four casualties of our busy lives – Creativity, Integrity, Levity and Love – can all bring soul enrichment, both to us and to others, when not neglected in our day-to-day journeys. Following are some suggestions on how to protect the external expression of ourselves so that being rich in soul is a reality and not just an aspiration.

"In the beginning God created the heavens and the earth."[67]
Written a seriously long time ago BC

"But unless we are creators, we are not fully alive.
What do I mean by creators? Not only artists, whose acts of creation are the
obvious ones of working with paint or clay or words. Creativity is a way of
living life, no matter what our vocation or how we earn our living. Creativity is
not limited to the arts or having some kind of important career."[68]
Madeleine L'Engle

Chapter 14

༄

Creativity

BEING CREATIVE IS ONE of the easiest things to neglect when you are time-poor (unless, of course, your job is as a professional designer, or you dance or sing for a living!). The problem with creativity is that it can feel like a holiday luxury or a school activity not to be indulged in by grown-ups.

However, there is something incredibly satisfying about creating something out of nothing – and most people can think of a creative idea they have suppressed through lack of opportunity.

Ilana

Ilana describes herself as an introvert by nature. She enjoys quiet time alone and gets stressed if she is in the company of others without a break. She completed her studies in maths and applied maths, chemistry and physics and became a sanitation engineer focussing on developing countries.

What takes people by surprise is to learn that when she was 10, Ilana asked her parents if she could join the local flower-arranging club. There were about 45 women over the age of 50 – and ten-year-old Ilana! Over the next four years, she learned every aspect of the art of flower arranging, and although she never won any of the competitions, she got many runner-up prizes and encouragement awards.

Ilana's hobby of arranging flowers eventually gave way to a passion for gardening – dealing with plants in the ground. She loved to consider the design and structure of gardens, and the combination of plants and colours. Perhaps a natural extension of this was a love of mosaic work and painting. When she got married in 1992, however, Ilana didn't paint for another 15 years – mainly because she was extremely busy with international travel and her work with global organisations, and because she and her husband were enjoying designing a garden for their newly purchased home in Melbourne, and later designing renovations to their house.

But after years of marriage, when the family was living in Jakarta in Indonesia, Ilana was facing a myriad of pressures at work. She was nearing breaking point. After a family holiday in the Northern Territory, she returned to work leaving her husband and son on a stop-over in Darwin; and the first night back at home she pulled out paints and a canvas. Each evening and all weekend, Ilana painted. She worked in acrylics with large splashes of colour – plenty of yellow and orange reflecting the colours of the desert she had just visited – and lots of abstract lines and dots inspired by the Australian Aboriginal art she had so enjoyed on her recent holiday. Once the paintings were finished, she hung them around her house.

Ilana found that the act of painting gave her incredible joy and peace. She loved the process of painting each tiny dot – one after another – in perfect rows of design. Ilana had not signed her name on any of the paintings, and when her husband got home, he just assumed she had bought the artwork to decorate the stark white walls. It was only some time later, when he asked where she had found the paintings, that she admitted she herself was the artist.

For her, it was the activity of painting that was therapeutic and not the acknowledgment from anyone else that they liked her work. In fact, when her husband, who loved the paintings, proceeded to tell all their visitors about their provenance, Ilana promptly moved most of the works out of the way.

Seeing Ilana's colourful handiwork on her study walls around her is a reminder of that other side to her life. Ilana gained incredible richness of soul from finding space to be creative – including flower arranging, garden design, mosaic work, interior design and painting.

Lisa

When I first went into legal recruitment, I hired Lisa, a woman who also loved to paint. Lisa painted the most exquisite portraits of women. Eventually she came to me to say she needed to resign from her job because she had no time to paint anymore (which was her real passion).

I quickly realised she would be willing to work part-time if we offered such an option, and we agreed to a new work arrangement. She would work for us in the mornings and in the afternoons go home to paint.

> "Creativity is oxygen for our souls. Cutting off our creativity makes us savage."[69]
>
> *Julia Cameron*

Lisa took the hard decision to forfeit financial gain for a season to pursue an artistic passion which gave her much greater rewards. Not everyone is able to express their creative gifts in a satisfying way whilst staying in full-time employment, and Lisa's decision to make more space in her life was her response to this dilemma.

Rebecca

Rebecca (the corporate lawyer from Chapter 2) had always dreamed of learning to paint. However, full-time work and three children kept her completely busy for many years. Eventually, as the children got older, she started to let her dream come back to the surface. She subscribed to a weekly email alert that notified her of social events in the city, and one day the email advertised an eight-week beginner's course in acrylic painting near her workplace. She immediately enrolled.

For Rebecca, her "60 second solutions" were to dream of the opportunity to paint and then to subscribe to the email service which advertised various opportunities. After this small beginning, her lengthier solution was to commit two hours a week for two months to do the course. And now Rebecca has a new "60 second solution" – she cuts out pictures from magazines which are the sorts of colours and scenes she would like to paint one day and pastes them into a scrapbook. This is her preparation for the lengthier project of one day painting a picture.

Zara

Zara has been creating music and songs since she was a teenager. Her gift is extraordinary – sometimes she wakes up with a whole song swirling around her head, both the music and lyrics. She is always looking for a scrap of paper to write her music down as it comes to her, and once she had to resort to writing on toilet paper from a nearby bathroom. For years she kept a tape recorder in her car, but these days she tries to remember to carry her dictaphone with her.

"Creativity gives hope that there can be a worthwhile idea. Creativity gives the possibility of some sort of achievement to everyone. Creativity makes life more fun."[70]

Edward de Bono

Zara has two Bachelor's degrees and two Master's degrees, and she has worked in many different places in both the education sector and hospitality. But when asked where her joy and soul enrichment have come from over the years, she immediately starts to sing one of her songs. Zara not only loves creating music; she also believes that music itself is creative as it produces mood and joy and mystery. She has found that music lifts her out of any spot she is in, and she also uses it to highlight what she believes is important in life.

Zara's brother was a millionaire businessman whose money began to rule his life. When he and his second wife died in an air crash, his two children inherited all his wealth. Zara was saddened to see that this money brought strife rather than joy to her niece and nephew. In fact, her nephew was eventually millions of dollars in debt and bankrupt. Zara finds it heartening to challenge the norm of materialism through her music.

Gayle

Gayle (the horse riding radiologist from Chapter 12) has a specific creative outlet that helps her connect with her children at the same time. Years ago, she committed to making a single-bed quilt cover for each of her three children. She enjoys the discipline of sewing small squares together, and she has involved each of her kids in deciding on colours and fabric. Gayle tells me she has just finished her son's quilt cover and it took a full three years! She certainly enjoyed the process, and it is a gift that enriches her children as well.

Bonnie

Bonnie is the school teacher described in Chapter 12. Early on, she adopted the strategy of learning something new every year. She has studied Japanese, undertaken singing lessons, learnt to sew swimwear and lingerie, and taken on a number of other craft courses – including quilting. Apparently she did not enjoy the quilting! However, the adventure of exploring new creative outlets has enriched Bonnie's soul.

✧

Whilst quilting and crafts often give joy to their creators, I personally feel terrified at the thought of engaging in these activities. I confess I once volunteered to lead a "non-knitters union" at a church women's camp, and my cheeky stance inspired another like-minded attendee to promptly launch the "anti-quilting club"! I was not wanting to discourage those who love to be crafty; I just wanted to provide an alternative for women who might be more like me. So instead of reluctantly going to a craft workshop, I offered a poetry-writing workshop, which ended up being very well attended. I still receive beautiful cards from one of the women, who shares with me the wonderful haiku poems she keeps writing.

The kind of creativity that gives us joy will vary wildly amongst women, and I am convinced that no single activity is more worthy than another. But it is natural to be creative if we are surrounded by a wonderful, colourful and amazing creation. For the time-poor amongst us, there are a couple of simple ways to encourage our creativity, such as subscribing to alerts about our creative passion, or keeping a notebook where we brainstorm or sketch in moments of inspiration throughout the day. It is in such small beginnings that creative projects can take root and begin to blossom.

60 Second Solutions to Re-engage with Creativity

1. *Recall Significant Incidents:*
   - From your childhood, what creative activity gave you joy? Ponder if you would like to return to that creative activity.
   - From your current circumstances, what example of creativity inspires you and gives you hope for the future? Consider how you can encourage this creativity in yourself.

2. *Review Your Workplace:*
   - Place something in your car, on your desk or on a nearby wall that reflects your creativity – either something you have made or a photograph of it.
   - Tell your boss or colleagues about your favourite creative projects.
   - Look for opportunities to print an amusing award certificate from the internet to give to a colleague.
   - Volunteer for any work tasks that use some of your creative skills (for instance, designing a newsletter or joining the committee in charge of a new office fit-out).
   - Establish a fund to buy artwork for the organisation.
   - Bring a pot plant to work and remember to water it.

- Propose a competition in local schools where children write or draw something that connects them with your organisation.

3. *Resolve for the Future:*
   - Decide what creative activity you are going to indulge in.
   - Decide what you are going to say no to in order to start a new project.
   - Decide to subscribe to alerts about the creative area that is your passion.

4. *Research and Imagine:*
   Search the internet for information on:
   - online courses in singing, oil painting, short-story writing, gardening, candle making, knitting, sketching, scrapbooking, photobook making, guitar playing, piano playing, harp playing, stamp collecting, bird watching, juggling, acting, jewellery making, flower arranging, pottery making, curry cooking, cake cooking, camp cooking, blog writing, website designing, leather working, sculpturing, wood carving, ballroom dancing, belly dancing, foreign language learning, public speaking, hair cutting, dog grooming, origami making, calligraphy writing, engine building, short film making, photography, astronomy, wine appreciation, cake decoration, family history investigation, antiques collection, YouTube video creation, etc.

5. *Record in Your Notebook or on Your Electronic Device:*
   - Draw quick sketches; write haiku poems; brainstorm the plot of your first novel; draw quick plans of your garden make-over; write down that melody that's been floating around your head; list the birds or plants you see on your way to and from work.
   - Record the date you want to attend a course that will teach you more about a hobby you would like to pursue.
   - Record a list of the things you will need to purchase to get started on a hobby at home.

6. *Reach Out to Others:*
   - Contact a friend who has the same creative interest as you, and suggest it is time to join forces to be creative together.
   - Contact a tutor or instructor who can guide you in refining your creative skills.
   - If passing on a personal note to a friend, fold it into an origami animal first.
   - If encouraging someone, quote them a relevant poem or words from a famous leader, and then email the same message later.

7. *Refocus with a Time-Poor Prayer:*
   - Thank you God that you created the world and everything beautiful around us. Please help me to use the creative side of myself that I've been neglecting. Please remind me to plan ahead to use my creative gifts. Inspire my soul.

8. *Rest for 60 Seconds:*
   - Stop everything; think of something in creation you are grateful for right now; and rest in the knowledge that you are free to imagine.

Lengthier Remedies

- Write a poem; write a song; write a melody; write a symphony; write a short story; create a blog; design a website; map your family history; write a self-help book on how to write a book when you are time-poor!
- Paint a picture; sketch a scene or a person; make some candles; make some jewellery; design a leather wallet; make a pot out of clay; sculpture something out of rock or wood or watermelon.
- Join a choir; join a band; form a band; attend a ballroom dancing evening; join an acting class; cut someone's hair; cut someone's dog's hair.
- Cook something you haven't made since you were a kid; go wine

tasting; decorate a cake for a friend's birthday; attempt to juggle in front of your children.

- Join an astronomy club; join a bird-watching club; join a flower-arranging club; join a public-speaking club; join a book club; join a writing club.
- Dig up a part of your garden; plant something in that part of your garden; keep watering that part of your garden.
- Knit a scarf; make a scrapbook; take some photos; create a photobook; start a stamp album; learn a foreign language.
- Meet with a friend once a month to have a meal and indulge in your creative interest.
- Read the subtitles to all of the art works in an exhibition at a gallery.
- Read *The Artist's Way: A Course in Discovering and Recovering Your Creative Self* by Julia Cameron (Pan Books, 1995).

"The truly scary thing about undiscovered lies is that they have
a greater capacity to diminish us than exposed ones. They erode our strength,
our self-esteem, our very foundation."[71]
Cheryl Hughes

"They're certainly entitled to think that, and they're entitled to full respect
for their opinions...but before I can live with other folks I've got to live with
myself. The one thing that doesn't abide by majority
rule is a person's conscience."[72]
Atticus Finch

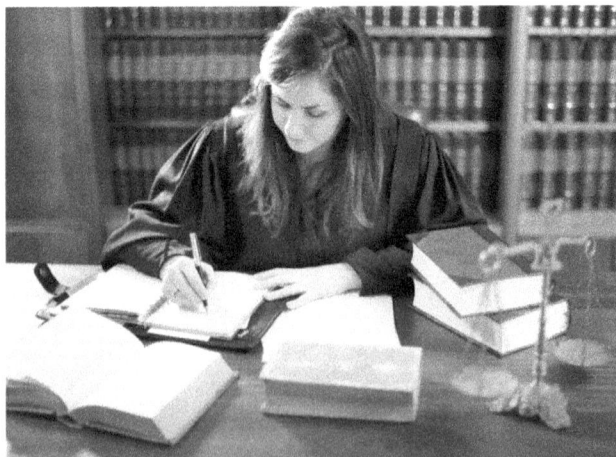

Chapter 15

ॐ

Integrity

IF YOU STRUGGLE PHILOSOPHICALLY with the idea that there are moral absolutes in the world, then consider the following scenarios. What do you say to the sex-slave trafficker who claims there is nothing wrong with snatching young girls from their villages to sell to wealthy customers since it is not personal but just a commercial business venture servicing a community need? What do you say to the man who has sex with a young child, knowing he is breaking the law, when he claims that he loves the child, or alternatively, that he legitimately paid for the service? What do you say to the internet scam artist who claims there is no ethical issue involved in sending out thousands of emails and successfully extracting money from willing but naive donors?

These perpetrators of wrongdoing may well claim to be enriched by their actions, but it is a counterfeit richness. Arguably, they are actually poisoning and corrupting their souls. Nearly every religion in the world has some version of the "golden rule" in its teachings: that we should treat others as we would like them to treat us.

Acting with integrity can often be a split-second decision. It can make the difference between a healthy heart and mind, and a compromised conscience that leaches away our joy.

Trudy

Trudy did not expect to go to prison for eight months. Her intention had been to keep her clients happy by solving their most pressing problem. She had not stolen anybody's money for her own gain. But she had decided to redirect funds that were earmarked for a different purpose. Instead of passing on the money given to her to invest, she made the ill-fated decision to use the money as dividends to appease her discontented clients. She broke the law and within four years was in a women's prison in Queensland.

Trudy was under pressure, and she let her integrity be compromised. Being time-poor or being stressed are both states that increase the chance of our losing perspective and making a bad choice which diverts our moral compass. It is often a decision made under pressure that is briefly appealing as a short-term solution.

Trudy was the most unlikely of criminals. Her parents were pastors of a local church, and she was happily married with three beautiful daughters. She had always lived a Christian life and gone out of her way to help others and live with integrity. In fact, when she was in prison, the other inmates called her a "straighty" because she was so obviously straight up and down in her approach to life and to the people around her.

Trudy had an early career in photography and sales, then later became a full-time investor and philanthropist. She specialised in property investment, but when she got interested in the share market, she looked for someone who knew more about the area than herself. She met a currency trader who had gained approval from ASIC to set up a registered managed fund. Trudy began the process of becoming his authorised representative. Her job was to receive funds from investors and pass them on to the currency trader for investing in the market. He was not interested in dealing with multiple individuals, so Trudy was the contact point for all investors.

This currency trader was incredibly effective and was able to promise very decent returns every month. After more than a year of getting such profitable returns, the investors became disturbed when the currency trader had a bad month and asked them to wait for returns, with interest, in the following month. However, the next month continued to be unprofitable in the currency trading business, and the investors once again had no returns.

Even though their returns had never been guaranteed, Trudy was suddenly inundated with calls from dissatisfied investors in various stages of panic. She started to feel ill every time she walked near her office. She knew there would be frantic emails and voice messages from people demanding their money back or asking for information she did not have. Trudy was finding it hard to contact the currency trader, and when she did speak with him, there was never enough information to appease the concerned investors.

Then the third month approached and the currency trader informed her he had once again failed to make enough money to provide a return to the investors. Trudy was becoming desperate to help all the people who

> "The highway of the upright is to depart from evil; He who keeps his way preserves his soul."[73]
>
> *King Solomon*

had entrusted their savings to her. She thought of an interim measure she believed would buy some time while the currency trader was trying to regain his profits. She had received new funds to be invested, but she decided, just this once, to distribute this money back to the investors as their monthly payment, and that way give some relief to the many people who were waiting for their regular payments to resume.

Trudy broke the law. She paid money to investors that had been given to her in trust to be invested. She lost everything in the subsequent liquidation. Four years later, she was sentenced to eight months in prison.

What Trudy did not know was that her currency trader was not what he seemed. He was actually a scam artist and a thief. He had never invested the money she passed on to him each month but had stolen it all. He also went to prison, and no one was surprised. But even the prosecutor was taken aback when the judge gave Trudy a sentence of eight months.

While serving her sentence, Trudy had plenty of time to think about the consequences of letting her integrity be compromised. She did not make the same mistake in prison. She took very seriously the moral obligation not to dob on her fellow inmates. In fact, she cared very much for the women she met inside – a mix of drug addicts, prostitutes and those who were convicted of more serious crimes, including murder.

The prison system tried to force the women to report each other for the smallest of infringements. Trudy decided immediately that refusing to become a snitch was actually an important part of keeping her integrity while in prison. Likewise, she did not allow the prison bullies to dictate who she would be kind to. There was one vulnerable Aboriginal woman who was ostracised by the other women due to her prickly personality – but Trudy went out of her way to be kind to this girl.

Trudy now warns women about the ways money can cause lapses of judgment in otherwise honest operators. One of the pieces of advice she gives is that busy women need to have strong boundaries so that priorities cannot be manipulated by others and judgment clouded. She also warns that we should keep ourselves in contact with trusted advisers. One of her biggest mistakes was to leave herself no one to confide in; her pastor, her accountant and her lawyer were all investing through her with the currency trader.

Trudy has also identified in herself a personality trait that did not assist her to keep a straight line. She says that by nature she was a "people pleaser" and a "martyr". These characteristics meant her longing for approval and her desire to help solve the problems of those coming to her in distress led her to choose an illegal course of action instead of finding a way which maintained her integrity and kept within the law.

Trudy found that many women were in prison because they felt they had no choice but to go along with their loved one's wrongdoing, or they had acted illegally after being subjected to domestic violence.

Georgia

When Georgia first became a management consultant, her boss used to give her tips on how to be successful, including the occasional instruction to lie to her clients. Georgia chose not to follow this advice. She thanked him for his concern and proceeded to work a little differently. Before long, Georgia was the most effective consultant in the business, and her boss publicly acknowledged this to the other staff. He said that Georgia did things "differently" – but he admitted it seemed to work!

> "Integrity is doing the right thing, even when no one is watching."[74]
>
> *C.S. Lewis*

Georgia's view is that telling the truth is the only honourable way to treat a client. When she explains this to colleagues who do not share her values, she just points out the need to think ahead to the worst-case scenario. Her view is that it is inevitable a client will eventually discover a deception, and when this happens, the client will never again trust that consultant. She values her reputation more highly than this, and she has found that her relationships are far more satisfying (and soul enriching) when they are based on honesty.

Georgia does not claim to be perfect. Whilst she was not susceptible to telling lies to her clients, she did increasingly find she was vulnerable to the flattery of her clients. More than one CEO told her over the years that he and his wife lived "separate lives" and were "drifting apart". Georgia loved her husband, but the more she was consumed by work, the more she found herself dwelling on the attentions of her interested clients. It was only when one of them took her to lunch in a hotel with rooms upstairs that she finally realised she had let her boundaries slide too far and needed to send clearer messages to the men she worked with.

ॐ

It is common to hear that money, sex and power can become obsessions to any of us when we are not careful. If we are seeking the soul enrichment that comes from keeping our integrity intact, then it is useful to be conscious of our weaknesses before we put ourselves in highly pressured situations. We are less likely to disappoint ourselves (and potentially to break the law) if we already have boundaries and principles in place. We will also protect ourselves if we remain accountable to one or more trusted advisers.

Another useful thing to remember is that not one of us is perfect. We all make mistakes. But there is a very powerful remedy to failure. The simple acts of saying sorry to our creator and to those we have wronged, and asking for forgiveness, are soul enriching actions in themselves.

60 Second Solutions to Re-engage with Integrity

1. *Recall Significant Incidents:*
   - From your childhood, recall a good decision that made you feel right in your soul, and ponder how to keep your conscience clear.
   - From your current circumstances, think of a situation where you were in danger of compromising or breaking the law (or where you actually did wrong) and consider how to guard against such situations in the future.

2. *Review Your Workplace:*
   - Tell the truth (or say nothing) when tempted to lie.
   - Be honest about what matters to you when asked, or when you have the chance to speak up.
   - Offer to pay for company resources when using them for your own purposes.
   - Be vigilant about the messages you give people who are potentially attracted to you (or whom *you* are attracted to).
   - Apologise when you cause grief to another.

3. *Resolve for the Future:*
   - Decide that when you are undercharged or given too much change in a shop, you will tell the shop assistant and right the wrong.
   - Decide in advance how you will deal with ethical issues at work.

4. *Research and Imagine:*
   Search the internet for information on:
   - stories of good Samaritans
   - lessons learned from the collapse of Enron
   - key principles of business ethics
   - the Ten Commandments.

5. *Record in Your Notebook or on Your Electronic Device:*
   - Collect famous quotes on business ethics.
   - Record the names of your key trusted advisers.

6. *Reach Out to Others:*
   - Contact a person you have wronged to apologise, offer restitution and ask forgiveness.
   - Contact a wise mentor, and suggest that you catch up to discuss any pressing ethical dilemmas.

7. *Refocus with a Time-Poor Prayer:*
   - Thank you God that you are truly good. Please help me to live with integrity and to know right from wrong. Please help me to treat others as I would like them to treat me. Protect my soul.

8. *Rest for 60 Seconds:*
   - Stop everything; think of something good you are grateful for right now; and rest in the knowledge that God forgives us for our shortcomings, wrongdoings and failings.

Lengthier Remedies

- Watch the documentary about the fall of Enron: *Enron: The Smartest Guys in the Room.*
- Watch the movie *Chocolat* and consider the difference between legalism and integrity.
- Conduct an audit of your own core values and consider how you want to live in relation to them.
- Read *Integrity: The Courage to Meet the Demands of Reality* by Dr Henry Cloud (HarperCollins, 2006).

"God grant me a vacation to make bearable what I can't change. A friend to make it funny. And the wisdom to never get my knickers in a knot because it solves nothing and just makes me walk weird!"[75]
Anonymous

"There is a time for everything, and a season for every activity under the heavens... A time to weep and a time to laugh, a time to mourn and a time to dance."[76]
An Ancient Jewish Teacher

Chapter 16

၅

Levity

I ONCE VISITED MOSCOW and was shocked by how few people ever smiled. My next destination after Russia was Sweden – and the contrast was dramatic. Laughing, grinning and smiling people were everywhere. I pondered this difference for many months until I met someone who told me of a Russian friend who had left Moscow to live with them abroad. Apparently, living under communist rule for so many years had created a culture of fear and disaffection, and the experience of this Russian friend was that her face muscles were so unaccustomed to smiling that it took her a number of months to gain the ability to smile naturally.

In Anne Holm's novel *I am David*, David had no experience of people smiling in the prison camp where he spent his first 12 years. When he escaped, he saw lots of laughing and smiling, and because he knew he looked strange to others, he tried to get himself to smile. However, no matter how much he tugged at his lips and mouth, he could not get his face to conform to the same sort of happy expression he could see on the faces of others. It was only after saving a beautiful little girl from a fire that David found himself smiling with her in joy. He then realised that smiling was associated with happiness.

Being able to laugh and smile, and having a light heart, certainly appears to be a good medicine for our souls.

Lynette

If an example of embracing levity is encouraging humour in our lives, then Lynette has certainly succeeded. Lynette is the successful deputy principal and business woman described in Chapter 2, and when she is on yard duty, she goes out of her way to find things to laugh at with the students, rather than looking for someone breaking the rules.

Lynette lightens her weekend by listening to cricket and football in the background when at home, and if she can find a willing friend, she will put on her Adelaide Crows scarf (and poncho if it is raining) and attend a football game. Joining in the jocularity of the crowd gives Lynette great pleasure, and if her team loses, she is happy to become the subject of gentle ribbing from the winners when she gets back to school on Monday.

Lynette refuses to take herself too seriously, and as a result she keeps herself light-hearted and adds laughter to the lives of others.

Lily

No one would have guessed that Lily cried every day before going to work. She was good at putting on a positive public face, and her clients all loved her.

Lily had been running her own financial planning business for ten years after being a successful accountant for her first five years out of university. She had chosen the financial planning business because she loved helping people. The only problem was that she hated her job! Not her clients – she adored her clients – but she hated the work and the business side of things. She was additionally stressed because she had spent years unsuccessfully trying to have a baby with her husband. She could not remember the last time she laughed.

Lily had laughed a lot as a child. Having fun and playing hilarious games had come naturally to her. However, she was also a "gifted child", and it wasn't long before there was a conflict between her light-hearted nature and her obligation to succeed in her studies. Lily could read at the age of three, and when she tried to read *Pride and Prejudice* at the age of six, the nuns at her Catholic school confiscated the novel and returned it to the library. Suddenly there were rules about the best way for her to learn, and Lily was not enjoying the process.

Also, she quickly realised that being a gifted child did not attract friends in the schoolyard, but rather made her a target for bullying and mockery. So she tried to bring back some fun by becoming the class clown. This certainly guaranteed her more friends, but it created a divide between the "gifted Lily", who had to be serious (and whose singing was criticised by the nuns), and the "fun Lily", who could always find joy by subverting the system.

"A cheerful heart is a good medicine, but a downcast spirit dries up the bones."[77]

King Solomon

Eventually the weight of academic obligation prevailed over Lily's good humour, and she dutifully enrolled in commerce and arts at university. It was really the music and drama she loved most rather than the dry accounting, but she persevered with both courses of study. Then inevitably the pressure to "get a real job" stopped her from pursuing a career in singing or performance, and she joined a large accounting firm. She was very good at everything she put her hand to (that's the trouble with growing up as a gifted child), and after a number of successful roles with big corporate employers, she set up the financial planning firm.

Her business thrived, but Lily was fading away. Somehow she felt she had lost her way. She had stopped singing and laughing, and somehow she had lost her faith along the way as well.

Finally she reached out for professional help and managed to make sense of her situation with the help of a talented psychologist. She realised she had stopped living authentically and was trying to live the life others expected of her. In fact, she had got to the point where she avoided catching up with friends because she found it exhausting always putting on a show and a brave face.

In order to help lighten the day for herself and her staff at work, Lily introduced a five-minute coffee game where everyone came together and someone was given permission to "have a whiffle". A whiffle is where you can speak briefly about anything that comes to mind – it is "what I feel like expressing". The goal is to make your colleagues chuckle, so you might chat about burning the toast at breakfast, or your cat's propensity for climbing the curtains.

With encouragement from her new mentor, Lily decided to go on a retreat and do some serious self-reflection. She quickly realised her financial planning business was actually hurting her soul. She thought long and hard about the things she was truly passionate about, and she kept coming back to music, children and social justice. She also realised that she wanted to rediscover her spiritual side.

> "The only way to get through life is to laugh your way through it. You either have to laugh or cry. I prefer to laugh. Crying gives me a headache."[78]
>
> *Marjorie Pay Hinkley*

Lily decided to sell her business and enrol in a new university course to prepare her to teach music to children. Having finally given birth to her own child, Lily's desire to work with gifted children in the field of music and dance became even clearer. Once she had started her Master's degree in early childhood education, far from crying each day, Lily found she was skipping to university. And she had finally found her "laugh" again.

For Lily, the loss of levity in her life had been a long slow process, and a highly soul destroying journey. She has taken drastic measures to restore the joy to her life and family. Hopefully, many of us can restore some light-heartedness to our days – without having to dispense with our businesses or resign from our jobs.

ക

Sometimes it can come down to a split-second decision when you choose to laugh rather than despair over something. My husband and I recently had a teenager staying with us, and I accidentally spilt a jug of milk across the kitchen bench and onto the floor at his feet. I instantly grinned and said, "Let's not cry over spilt milk", then cracked-up laughing at my own hilarious joke.

My young friend was shocked. He had been expecting me to swear or get frustrated – and he couldn't understand why I wasn't getting angry. In fact, he was so confused that he commented on the fact he had seen me laugh more than once when something went wrong.

I then realised that, whenever possible, my habit *is* to laugh rather than let myself become irritated by life. Sometimes maintaining our richness of soul is a matter of controlling our reactions to things. Laughing at life's small irritations rather than cursing is a way of preventing stress from creeping up on us and getting the better of us.

60 Second Solutions to Re-engage with Levity

1. *Remember Significant Incidents:*
   - From your childhood, what event made you laugh from your belly? Consider where to find similar levity today.
   - From your current circumstances, what prospect puts a skip in your step and a smile on your face? Ponder how to increase this response.

2. *Review Your Workplace:*
   - Recognise opportunities to create a moment of joy for your colleagues.
   - Take a cup of coffee to a work-mate and invite them to "have a whiffle".
   - When you and a colleague are heading for a stressful meeting, suggest a game of 60-second bingo: you choose three things that you have to find in your surroundings, and the first to find them wins (for example, a briefcase, a bald man and the colour purple).
   - Sing a line from one of your favourite songs each time you arrive at work.
   - Rotate various posters near your desk which give some amusing advice for the day (two of my favourites are: "If you are going through hell – keep going" and "You can't have everything. Where would you put it?").

3. *Resolve for the Future:*
   - Decide that whenever you do an activity with others, you will always ask yourself how to add some fun to it.
   - Decide that if you have to do a difficult job, you will make it more fun by eating your favourite food at the same time, or if possible by doing the job in a place you love such as in a fern garden.
   - Decide that when something irritating happens, you will laugh and recite a witty comment to amuse yourself.

4. *Research and Imagine:*
   - Find and watch a funny YouTube clip relating to your favourite animal (funny puppies; funny bears; funny penguins; funny mice; funny kittens; funny meerkats; funny monkeys; funny otters; etc.).

   Search the internet for:
   - funniest jokes; funniest cartoons; funniest movies of all time; best-ever quick board games
   - images of funniest looking dogs; weird-looking houses.

5. *Record in Your Notebook or on Your Electronic Device:*
   - Write a list of your favourite jokes.
   - Make a list of fun things you can do with children when they are driving you crazy (like putting on some music and dancing with them).
   - Record a list of the things you are passionate about which give you joy – and write suggestions as to how engage with those things.

6. *Reach Out to Others:*
   - Contact someone who enjoys a joke and share your favourite giggle.
   - Contact someone who needs a laugh and arrange to watch a comedy with them.
   - Contact someone who loves to organise a party, and suggest they host a fancy dress dinner party with you as a guest.

7. *Refocus with a Time-Poor Prayer:*
   * Thank you God that you have a sense of humour. After all, you did design the platypus, and look at how you've made me! Please help me to lighten my days, and please help me to laugh more. Cheer my soul.

8. *Rest for 60 Seconds:*
   * Stop everything; think of something amusing you are grateful for; and rest in the knowledge that joy can turn up unexpectedly.

Lengthier Remedies

   * Buy a new board game and find a friend to play with you over coffee, lunch or dinner one day.
   * Watch a funny movie with a friend.
   * Send a funny greeting card to a friend.
   * Go to a class to learn rock 'n' roll dancing.
   * Read *I Don't Know How She Does It* by Allison Pearson (Vintage Books, 2003).

"...Love is not love
Which alters when it alteration finds,
Or bends with the remover to remove:
O, no! it is an ever-fixèd mark,
That looks on tempests and is never shaken..."[79]
William Shakespeare

"The greatest disease in the West today is not TB or leprosy;
it is being unwanted, unloved, and uncared for. We can cure physical
diseases with medicine, but the only cure for loneliness, despair,
and hopelessness is love."[80]
Mother Teresa

Chapter 17

❧

Love

SOME WOULD ARGUE THAT LOVE is the ultimate "60 second solution". After all, it "makes the world go round"! It is in loving others and being loved ourselves that we find some of our richest moments. An act of love might be as simple as choosing not to turn our back and slam a door when we are frustrated or angry with someone close to us. My husband and I have decided that the most powerful demonstration of love is to be kind to one another.

Love and kindness are certainly easy to neglect when we are stretched with many competing pressures. But the soul enrichment that comes (to both parties) from remembering to be kind is worth the self-discipline.

Kate

Some people seem to be better at love than others. When I was growing up on the family farm, I really didn't think about the fact that the sheep in our paddocks one day ended up as lamb chops on our dinner table. But my little sister Kate loved all the animals on the farm, so when "Chrissy the calf" ended up as sausage meat, Kate was in tears.

Kate is a true "heart person". She still loves her pets in the same way, she loves her friends and she loves her hairdressing clients. She doesn't just chat to them aimlessly; she is concerned about their well-being and lives. One example of Kate's love for her clients is that she uses the more expensive, good-quality products. She knows that many of her competitors use the cheapest products to increase their profits whilst neglecting the nourishment of their clients' hair.

When she was younger, Kate also looked forward to loving some babies, but for years she could not get pregnant. Finally she and her husband had a beautiful baby boy, and a number of years later she was pregnant with a girl. But this time the doctors recommended she abort the baby because the foetus had a malformed heart. Kate could never consider this response, and she looked at all the alternatives. In the end the baby was born and had three heart operations in the first week of her life. She is now a healthy five-year-old, and as gorgeous and feisty as any little girl in the playground! The love my sister had for this little baby in her womb, and the continuous love she pours out on her friends and family, continues to be a blessing to all.

In the days when Kate had no children she had more time to express her love through concrete actions. There was one elderly lady who had very few visitors, and Kate made a habit of visiting her once every week. These days her plate is full with a husband, three children and a busy hairdressing business, so she finds other ways to express her love. She sponsors "heart kids" in Australia and funds a "sponsored child" overseas. She makes sure she cuddles her kids as often as possible, and she regularly tells them how much she loves them. When she has a friend in need, Kate will usually text them from her phone to express her concern.

> "Where there is love, there is life."[81]
>
> *Mahatma Gandhi*

Milly

Milly is another "heart person" – someone whose ability to love and empathise with others is evident to all who meet her. It is easy to be enriched by Milly. Her friends, colleagues and clients always feel she has their best interests at heart. She is interested in them and cares about them. Milly loves them all.

During her final year at high school in Brisbane, Milly's parents were in the process of separating. Milly had always been a high-achieving student and she soldiered on, eventually graduating from university and becoming a social worker, first in Brisbane and then in Sydney. She loved her work and she loved her clients, many of whom were from the most disadvantaged sectors of society. She fought for their rights and worked for their well-being. Often she had to intervene to protect children from abuse and neglect.

Despite her loving personality, for many years Milly felt incredibly poor in soul, as well as being time-poor. Because of her generous nature, she worked ridiculous hours and would fall asleep as soon as she got home, only to wake herself up to prepare for whatever child abuse case was running in court the next day. She was negotiating a demanding job, surviving a stressful marriage and navigating the comings and goings of two teenage stepchildren. After more than a decade of giving most of her life and energy to her work, Milly was burnt out. She resigned from her job, but this seemed too late for her marriage, which was also in meltdown mode.

In order to keep paying the bills, Milly chose to work in various casual and part-time jobs. It was only a few months after resigning from her social work career that Milly discovered she was pregnant with an unplanned child. Her husband's two children were nearly adults, and he was not impressed.

Milly was 40 years old, and she did not know how she would cope. But even she could not foresee the catastrophe that was approaching. Within three weeks of giving birth to her daughter, Milly was diagnosed with postpartum psychosis and was admitted to a psychiatric hospital for treatment. After a couple of weeks, she was allowed to have the baby with her, and she spent a further six weeks in the mother and baby unit of the hospital.

When her daughter was six months old, Milly left her rocky marriage and returned to her family in Brisbane for support. She loved her daughter, and as the months passed, Milly was able to deal with some unresolved issues in relation to her separated parents. Also, she slowly re-engaged with the community. She joined the school council and volunteered at a local NGO, eventually being hired full-time by them to work in administration. She enjoyed being able to contribute to the mental health sector, using her social work skills in a new way.

Finally, after a number of years, Milly's husband relocated to Brisbane to join her and their daughter, and they rebuilt their relationship on a new, more solid foundation. Milly put into practice some advice she had heard as a teenager: if you do the acts of love, then the feelings will follow. There was a new love and respect in her marriage, she had restored loving relationships with her parents, and she loved her workmates and clients as much as ever.

Despite being a particularly loving woman, Milly still found soul enrichment elusive. However, around this time she began to understand another aspect of love she had never fully experienced before. Milly learned the art of loving herself. She was a Christian and had always believed that God loved her. She understood the theological proposition that God had demonstrated his love for her by choosing to sacrifice his own son (Jesus) instead of requiring her to be judged for her own wrongdoing. She also believed that because of this love from God, she was his "beloved daughter". But still she felt poor in soul. Somehow Milly had always let negative self-talk about her inadequacies cripple her opinion of herself.

In her mid-40s, Milly learnt how to challenge and control her thoughts, and she prayed to God for freedom from her negativity. It worked. For what seemed like the first time in her life, she was not unhappy with herself. Despite blessing others with her loving nature, she was only able to bless herself when she finally started to truly love and not condemn herself. The irony is that throughout her life as a Christian, she had always believed that God did not condemn her. It was adopting this attitude that finally dissipated the sadness in her soul.

Love may seem easier for "heart people" who naturally feel strongly about everything, but even the most analytical "head person" can actively love others – primarily because love is not only a feeling but also a behaviour and a choice.

Love has undergone a difficult journey in modern times. Hollywood has made it into a virus that can take over a person's will and common sense, and turn them into an automaton who has no choice but to devote themselves to the source of the contagion. And as quickly as the love-virus consumes a person, it can disappear as if it never existed.

This type of "love" is a long way from Shakespeare's "never shaken" variety quoted above. There is certainly something wonderful about a love that is undeserved and never ceases, no matter what. Even when the feelings of love rise and fall with life's fluctuations, we can choose to be constant in our loving actions and attitudes.

Although we can make the choice to show love to others, we cannot be certain that other people will love us. Many people, however, will give lip-service to the idea that *God* loves us, even if few can articulate what God's love means or how it actually works.

> "Dear friends, let us love one another, for love comes from God... because God is love."[82]
>
> *The Apostle John*

The Bible says that one way to see God's love is by the fact he sent his son Jesus to die a sacrificial death for us all. Someone once accused Shakespeare of being "full of clichés", and it is not surprising that the story of Christianity seems to many to be the same, given that the Bible is the most published and read book in the world (and also the most shoplifted, according to my local bookstore manager). So we commonly hear that "Jesus died for us" or "we are saved by the blood of the lamb". This can sound pretty ridiculous to anyone without a knowledge of the Bible (or to someone like me who loves lamb chops!), but the cliché makes sense in the context of the Jewish tradition where a perfect lamb was sacrificed so that the wrongdoings of the people could be forgiven.

If God really does love us, then we have an excellent "60 second solution" at our disposal: pursuing the experience of that divine love.

60 Second Solutions to Re-engage with Love

1. *Remember Significant Incidents:*
   - From your childhood, recall a time when you experienced pure love, and ponder how to love others in this way.
   - From your current circumstances, recall an act of love you admire, and reflect on how to replicate this behaviour.

2. *Review Your Workplace:*
   - Remind your colleagues to love their clients rather than treat them as mere sources of profit.
   - Treat your colleagues, clients and management in the same way you would like them to treat you.

3. *Resolve for the Future:*
   - Decide that when your loved ones make mistakes, you won't keep a list of their wrongs.
   - Decide that when your loved ones want to do something different from your preference, you won't always insist on your own way.
   - Decide that you will love yourself as well as loving others.

4. *Research and Imagine:*
   Search the internet for information on:
   - inspiring love stories
   - the best love poems
   - the best love songs
   - the five love languages.

5. *Record in Your Notebook or on Your Electronic Device:*
   - Make a note of what "love language" you believe your family members and friends will best respond to.
   - Write out the definitions of "love" that appear in the Bible in Paul's first letter to the church at Corinth (*1 Corinthians* 13:4–8) and John's first letter (*1 John* 4:10), and reflect on them sometimes.
   - Make a list of ways you can enrich your family and friends with actions that make them feel loved.

6. *Reach Out to Others:*
   - Contact the person closest to you to tell them you love them.
   - Contact someone who knows something about the love of God, and arrange a time to meet and compare notes.
   - Regularly give your child a hug or cuddle.
   - Regularly bless your partner and friends with something you know they appreciate as an act of love (be it a physical touch, a gift, an act of service, a word of appreciation or some quality time).
   - Pick a flower and give it to a friend in need.

7. *Refocus with a Time-Poor Prayer:*
   - Thank you God that you are love. Thank you that your best demonstration of that was letting Jesus take the punishment we deserve for our wrongdoing. Please help me see how wide and deep your love is, and help me love others better. Revive my soul.

8. *Rest for 60 Seconds:*
   - Stop everything; think of some act of love you are grateful for right now; and rest in the knowledge that you are loved.

Lengthier Remedies

- Prepare and deliver a love feast or love outing for your family or friends.
- Attend a course which explores how God loves us.
- Write and send a love letter of encouragement to someone you care about.
- Keep a gratitude diary, and include the things you love about yourself and others.
- Read *The Five Love Languages: The Secret to Love that Lasts* by Gary Chapman (Northfield Publishing, 2010).

PART B

❧

Overcoming
Obstacles to
Soul Enrichment

I BELIEVE WE CAN STILL HAVE an inner contentment and a sense of wholeness and well-being despite having little if any discretionary time.

I have suggested that re-engaging with a number of soul enriching aspects of life can assist with this journey – if, in fact, our time-poor lives have caused us to neglect these things.

But it may be there is something else getting in our way. Soul enrichment can elude us not because we fail to live intentionally and mindfully, but for other reasons that are more about our personality traits, our mindset and our personal approach to life, success and suffering.

In the following chapters I explore ways of recognising and overcoming the obstacles that come from our own self-sabotage, our inconsistent viewpoints on life, and our response to loss. The final chapter is one woman's story on how she coped when she had "tried everything" and still felt there was something missing.

Chapter 18

༄

Self-Sabotage?
Five Pesky Personality Traits

SOMETIMES WE ARE OUR own worst enemy. We might have tried many of the strategies described so far in this book but still crave that elusive soul enrichment. Could it be that we are actively undermining ourselves?

Despite being chronically time-poor myself, I know I am partly to blame for my plight. I have the tendencies of a perfectionist and a control freak, and I have always been in danger of being a workaholic. The answers to this quick quiz may shed light on your particular brand of self-sabotage:

1. What do you fear most in the workplace?

(a)	Losing control
(b)	Not being liked or recognised
(c)	Making a mistake
(d)	Not being appreciated
(e)	Becoming a nobody who has nothing to deal with

2. What do you dislike most in the workplace?

(a)	Inefficiency
(b)	Disagreeable, boring colleagues

(c)	Shoddy work
(d)	Bullying
(e)	Having nothing to do

3. What primarily drives you in the workplace?

(a)	Pride in your outcomes and achievements
(b)	Pride in yourself
(c)	Pride in your procedural excellence
(d)	Pride in your business, company or corporation
(e)	Pride in how long you spend at work

4. What primarily wastes your time in the workplace?

(a)	Not delegating enough to others
(b)	Chatting to or emailing colleagues too often
(c)	Trying to get it perfect too often
(d)	Going the extra mile too often
(e)	Nothing wastes my time – everything I do is necessary

How did you score? Make a note of how many times you selected an answer from each of the following categories:

Score (a):   Score (b):   Score (c):   Score (d):   Score (e):

Your greatest flaw might well be indicated by the category you have chosen most often. Consider the self-sabotage profiles below which are suggested by each of the categories:

Category	Self-sabotage profile
Mostly scores of (a)	Control freak
Mostly scores of (b)	Attention seeker
Mostly scores of (c)	Perfectionist
Mostly scores of (d)	Martyr
Mostly scores of (e)	Workaholic

If you are anything like me, you are a combination of more than one of these profiles. At least one of my friends identifies with all five!

Just because we have a personality that tends towards one of these traits does not automatically mean we are sabotaging our well-being. However, without vigilance we can let our bad habits get out of control and hurt both ourselves and others. Self-sabotage can steal our time and numb our souls. Unfortunately, our bad habits can also open the door to other character weaknesses and fears that can escalate our self-sabotage to a whole new level.

All of these self-sabotaging tendencies are exhausting to sustain, and they all seem to have a root either in low self-esteem and the longing for approval, or in an extra strong ego and the tendency for disapproval. Having a rich soul can help free us from these traits, but ironically, it is these very traits that can sabotage our richness of soul. It is a wearying circle of soul diminishment. Below, I explore how each of these personality traits can undermine us, and I suggest 60 second solutions that might assist in liberating us.

The Control Freak

Stephanie

Stephanie project-managed her work and project-managed her marriage. She was a classic control freak, never leaving anything to chance.

Steph was the daughter of a high-achieving, entrepreneurial father. There was no room for failure in her childhood; rather, she was driven to achieve from the start. And achieve she did. She graduated with an English literature major in her arts degree, and she then completed a postgraduate degree in engineering and technology. This course provided a challenge as there were only three women amongst a class of 30 men. Steph then quickly rose to a national role in a multinational telecommunications company working in the field of corporate risk. She continued on through her 30s, gaining enormous success in her career.

However, Stephanie was frustrated by her inability to get pregnant with her husband. As failure was not an option for her, Steph naturally commenced a gruelling IVF program. After flying all over Australia each week, she would return home to find the optimum moment to execute the baby-making process. But she did not get pregnant. Instead her life unravelled, and her tightly controlled work ethic failed to deliver the results she was looking for in both her marriage and her business. Her commitment to managing everything to the highest standard did not give her satisfaction but cultivated the opposite – a constant underlying sense of deficiency.

Steph was finally forced to let go of the reins – and she was relieved by how much this improved her life and well-being. (Chapter 13 tells Stephanie's story.)

❦

A control freak is very familiar with messages such as "Winning is everything" and "No one can do it as well as me." The trouble with this way of thinking is that it burdens the control freak with far more responsibility than is necessary. It is time wasting and soul destroying. You can also end up being bossy and annoying – just ask my staff!

One of the virtues of an excellent manager is the ability to listen to others, to consider their views and to delegate. Delegating tasks and responsibilities requires a certain degree of grace – in other words, the willingness to have work completed in a way which is to the best of someone else's ability, but not as your clone. As long as you do not re-do all the tasks you delegate, it is going to free up your time and honour the abilities of those around you.

One of the core fears behind this personality trait is the fear of losing control. In fact, the extreme control freak can become angry or frustrated when they are losing sway in a situation. Fear and anger are inherently soul destroying, and can easily chip away at our serenity and peace of mind. I like to remember the old advice: "Do not let the sun go down on your anger."[83]

Another way for a control freak to redirect their energy in a soul enriching activity is to find someone to mentor. Becoming a mentor honours the fact that you have expertise to share, and it respects the one who is keen to learn. Of course, with mentoring, as with delegating, the control freak must resist the urge to shape their subject in their own image.

The Attention Seeker

Lily

Lily admits to being an attention seeker from childhood when being the performer and class clown was her way of surviving as a gifted child. She desperately wanted to be liked by others and not to be pushed around because she was different. Having concluded that being funny was more appealing than being smart, Lily danced, joked and kidded her way through her teenage years.

> "In the multitude of my anxieties within me, Your comforts delight my soul."[84]
>
> *The Psalmist*

However, for Lily it was extremely soul destroying to have her well-being dependent on the approval of others. Eventually she learned to live more authentically and not allow her attention-seeking side to rule her life. (Chapter 16 tells Lily's story.)

Julie

Julie's family included a very prominent Australian, and she frequently attended social functions and awards events connected with this heritage. She enjoyed the attention this brought her, and she always "glammed up" and arrived early to position herself to meet all the right people. She liked to be as visible as possible, and she felt this was where she rightfully belonged. She also enjoyed the kudos that came after completing her PhD, when she could put "Doctor" before her name.

However, Julie's attention-seeking streak had a self-destructive downside. If she was not placed on the same table as the key dignitaries, she was quite miffed. If her photo did not appear in the social pages, her ego took a battering. When she gave up her academic career to support her widowed daughter, she feared the anonymity of being just a grandma. Julie's desire to be the centre of attention undermined her sense of contentment because she was always striving to gain recognition from those around her.

Chapter 9 tells the story of the sudden death of Julie's husband and the demise of their business. Julie came to realise that no matter how hard she tried, she could not control the public perception of her reputation. It was only when she stopped striving to always be noticed in a positive light that she felt more at peace within herself. She also had to love herself more than she loved the titles that could appear before her name. When much of her life was stripped away, Julie found people loved and accepted her not because of what she had achieved, but for who she was.

§

An attention seeker is in danger of believing the messages "I'm OK if I'm loved and admired by others" and "Life isn't worth living unless I can hear applause." Taken to its extreme, this personality trait can be very demoralising. It is exhausting to constantly strive for recognition and affection, and the fear of rejection is soul destroying in itself.

Another problem with being an attention seeker is that it can feel very unsettling to lose our spot in the limelight, and of course it should be equally unsettling if our limelight forces others into the shadows. A great first step to being free of this obstacle is learning to be content in our own skin. We will also benefit from seeking out those friends who really know us – foibles and all – and valuing their friendship above that of others we need to impress.

The Perfectionist

Liang

Liang admits she was a perfectionist right from her high school years. She put enormous pressure on herself to do well in her academic studies, but she had a strong fear of failure. In order not to disappoint her family (or herself), she would never admit that she thought she had done well in an exam. She would always predict and expect the worst. Then when her results were excellent, she could feel surprisingly proud of her achievements.

Liang admits that her perfectionism was emotionally exhausting. She also says she had to keep an "eternal perspective" on things so that her worries and concerns did not flood back into her heart. (Chapter 10 tells Liang's story.)

Rebecca

Rebecca is the corporate lawyer who loves to cook, and she identifies herself as a perfectionist. To be honest, I would rather have a lawyer who is a perfectionist than one who thinks that "close enough is good enough"! However, Rebecca says that at times her perfectionism wakes her in the middle of the night and keeps her thinking and worrying for a few hours of sleepless stress. She calls these her "brain whizzing" nights. Sometimes she will suffer this for three or four nights in a row.

Rebecca has found that one way to get relief from these distractions is to get up, make a cup of tea and write down everything that is going around in her head. Often this activity will be just enough to allow her to go back to sleep. Another technique she uses is to think through the framework of her role and to get a good understanding of what her job entails. If her client has asked her to limit her time on

> "...we need to be able to acknowledge our vulnerabilities... It is in the process of embracing our imperfections that we find our truest gifts: courage, compassion, and connection."[85]
>
> *Brené Brown*

a task, then Rebecca will qualify her legal advice by explaining she has been asked to be brief, and what follows will be an overview only. In these ways Rebecca limits the exhaustion that comes from not letting go of things. (Chapter 2 tells Rebecca's story.)

೨

A perfectionist may find themselves internalising messages such as "Close enough is never good enough" and "I must never make a mistake." There is no doubt that a perfectionist will be more time-poor than nearly all of their colleagues because they have to spend more time satisfying their passion for perfection. They can also easily get anxious or worried through fear of making a mistake, and anxiety is one of the biggest threats to peace and inner calm.

The journey to freedom from the soul destroying side of perfectionism can be a difficult one. Certainly adopting a mentor and learning self-compassion are two key beginnings. Also, many perfectionists have learnt to rejoice in a mistake (because it leads to new learning) and so have freed themselves from the enslavement of this personality trait.

The Martyr

Milly

Milly specialised in martyrdom for many years of her life. When she was at university studying social work, she would happily spend time helping a friend who arrived in need on her doorstep rather than swot for an exam the next morning. She loved to be needed and she excelled in self-sacrifice. In many ways this was her undoing, because she was always stretched too thinly – and her world eventually imploded. Milly's final breakthrough happened when she learned to love herself as much as she loved others. (Chapter 17 tells Milly's story.)

Trudy

Trudy is the investor who went to prison for a lapse of judgment in relation to the use of investors' money. She admits she always had a tendency towards being a people pleaser from an early age. When business got difficult, her desire to keep her investors happy led her down a road that eventually resulted in her breaking the law. Trudy's martyr complex was not only stressful but ultimately self-destructive.

Since experiencing the devastating results of being a people pleaser in the wrong way, Trudy has reviewed the way she responds to the needs of others. She has now developed some much stronger boundaries to counter the destructive nature of this martyr side of her personality. (Chapter 15 tells Trudy's story.)

༺ঞ༻

A martyr might find themselves repeating "I'll do whatever it takes" and "Somebody has to do it, so it might as well be me." Clearly being a martyr means you are extra time-poor, because you usually choose to do extra duties even when they might be unnecessary. Equally, being a martyr can be soul destroying.

More often than not, a martyr is motivated by the desire to please others and to be appreciated for those efforts. Martyrs are often seeking affirmation for their suffering. To them there is nothing worse than being taken advantage of and not being appreciated when so much has been done to deserve it.

Another soul destroying element to being a martyr is the tendency to be consumed by guilt when you are not fulfilling the various duties that weigh on your shoulders. Arguably this guilt is ill-founded, but the debilitating nature of guilt means that it can easily eat away at your soul enrichment and wholeness of heart.

A first step towards freedom from the consequences of being an extreme martyr is to develop clear boundaries which you communicate to those around you. Another useful step is to develop a habit of forgiving yourself and loving yourself for who you are. Sometimes the biggest obstacle for a martyr is low self-esteem, which could be addressed through external professional assistance. We should never be afraid to call on others for help.

The Workaholic

Nalini

It was only when Nalini's father was dying, and still running his business from his hospital bed in his late 80s, that Nalini realised how much her workaholism was wrapped up with her desire to get approval from her dad.

Nalini grew up in a family of very high-achieving elders. Her father was a successful businessman in Sydney, and her grandfather was a major general who knew Lawrence of Arabia in Baghdad. Her grandmother was a successful doctor 80 years ago when women were unlikely to even have jobs, let alone jobs in medicine. Suffice to say that Nalini and both of her siblings have had very strong work ethics.

Nalini always functioned at a million miles an hour. Her work was the focus of her life and everything else had to fit around it. She felt unsettled when she was not working, and she felt driven to achieve in all of her work endeavours no matter how difficult the tasks. Nalini's lifestyle was unsustainable and ultimately exhausting.

> "...family, friends and love, ultimately matter...Yet, watching contemporary behaviour, how many of us act as if it were true?... Workaholism has become a badge of honour."[86]
>
> *Anne Manne*

Before she could change, Nalini needed to admit that she had an addiction to work. Only then was she able to take steps to break the obsession. She used a number of strategies including getting professional help, going on a silent retreat, filling in a gratitude journal each night, and learning to pause and breathe when her physical symptoms escalated. (Chapter 11 tells Nalini's story.)

ℒ

A workaholic may well be convinced that "You can achieve anything you put your mind to" and "Nothing matters more than doing this project." These sorts of messages have their root in the truth that work is good, but they ignore the fact that it can take over.

We can all get great satisfaction and soul enrichment from purely doing a good job in our work, be it paid or voluntary. But being a workaholic is not just "doing a good job"; it is thinking only about the job! There is something obsessive in the workaholic's life. It may be an obsession with achievement; it may be an obsession with status and promotion (the need to constantly "get ahead"); or it may just be an obsession with accumulating wealth. A famous cautionary word of wisdom warns: "The love of money is a root of all kinds of evil."[87]

Being a workaholic means being addicted to work in an unhealthy way. It means that work enslaves us rather than us choosing to work. It means we might lie to our loved ones or steal time from those who need us in order to get our "fix". It might mean we have lost sight of what is important and replaced it with a work-drug that gives us false highs and serious lows. It probably means that work has somehow taken on a life of its own and got way out of our control – and we've let it be so. And we like it!

If you are a workaholic, you probably know you are, and your friends and family are probably giving you the same message. No doubt you work through meals (report-reading at the table?), through social events (blackberry at the theatre?) and through exercise workouts (dictaphone at the gym?). Or perhaps you never go home to dinner, go to the theatre or go to the gym, nor even take holidays anymore. And you probably know what soul enriching things you neglect each day, and how you actively sabotage the soul enrichment that might come from living a different life.

> "Work is as much a basic human need as food, beauty, rest, friendship, prayer, and sexuality; it is not simply medicine but food for our soul."[88]
>
> *Timothy Keller*

One explanation for workaholism is that somehow our work has become our identity, and we fear losing that identity if work does not have a primary place in our lives. In effect, our job has become our idol – the thing we value above all else, the thing that fills our mind. Betty Friedan, the well-known American feminist, gave some cautionary advice to women who might get caught in this predicament, asking: "Should women simply replace the glorification of domesticity with the glorification of work as their life and identity?"[89]

Those of us who are workaholics need to find that peaceful place where we can be ourselves and love ourselves, whether we are working or not. Without this freedom, our soul enrichment will always be under threat from self-sabotage. Self-reflection and self-awareness are excellent steps towards recognising and admitting our particular weaknesses. Becoming accountable to others who will give us support, and asking for help from God, are applicable strategies used in other situations of addiction.

But workaholism is not really like classic substance addictions. Work is not something we need to abstain from to break its enslavement. Rather, we need to put work into a healthy place in our lives. It is then we will be able to receive the joy that comes from doing a good job, and also the soul enrichment that comes from restored relationships with others and the increased care we can give ourselves.

60 Second Solutions to Disengage from Self-Sabotage

1. *Recall Significant Incidents:*
   - From your childhood, think about what soul destroying personality traits were exhibited by those around you, and consider whether you have adopted similar traits.
   - From your current circumstances, identify others who are similar to you, and consider how they prevent themselves from lapsing into extreme behaviour which is soul destroying.

2. *Review Your Workplace:*
   - Identify at what times and in what circumstances at work you are most susceptible to becoming a control freak, an attention seeker, a perfectionist, a martyr and/or a workaholic, and consider how to circumvent these habits.
   - Intentionally act in a manner which reverses your negative obsessions.

3. *Resolve for the Future:*
   - Decide that you will not let your soul destroying tendencies get out of hand.
   - Decide to explore the health of your self-esteem and ego, and to consider how to change any feelings of unworthiness or superiority that oppress you.
   - Decide what things matter most in life, and resolve how you want to prioritise your life according to those values.

4. *Research and Imagine:*
   Search the internet for information on:
   - how to stop being a control freak, attention seeker, perfectionist, martyr and/or workaholic.
   - how to say no.
   - how to set good boundaries.

5. *Record in Your Notebook or on Your Electronic Device:*
   - Write a list of tips on how to behave differently in the future.
   - Write a list of the health implications of not changing your behaviour.
   - Write a list of comforting quotes such as "Wanting to be someone else is a waste of the person you are"; or "He satisfies the longing soul, and fills the hungry soul with goodness".

6. *Reach Out to Others:*
   - Reach out to a trusted friend and ask them to help you keep accountable in relation to your self-sabotaging weaknesses.

- Tell people around you that you are trying to become less of a control freak, attention seeker, perfectionist, martyr and/or workaholic.
- Speak to a counsellor or pastor about how to reduce fear and restore worthiness within.

7. *Refocus with a Time-Poor Prayer:*
   - Forgive me God! I am sorry I have let myself become a control freak / attention seeker / perfectionist / martyr / workaholic to my own detriment (and no doubt to the grief of those around me).
   - For the control freak: Please free me from the need to always control everything in my life, and help me to look more to you for wisdom and calm.
   - For the attention seeker: Please free me from the need to always be liked and noticed in my life, and help me to look more to you for affirmation.
   - For the perfectionist: Please free me from the need to always be right in my life, and help me to look more to you for peace and forgiveness.
   - For the martyr: Please free me from the need to always be appreciated for everything I do, and help me to look more to you for boundaries.
   - For the workaholic: Please free me from the need to always be busy in my life, and help me to look more to you for my identity, rest and restoration.
   - Please send people to help me, angels to protect me, your Spirit to restore me and your love to redeem me. Renew my soul.

8. *Rest for 60 Seconds:*
   - Stop everything; think of something unrelated to work that you are grateful for right now; and rest in the knowledge that "busy" is not forever and the season will eventually change.

Lengthier Remedies

- Make an appointment to see a counsellor, pastor or psychologist to discuss your more extreme personality traits.
- Do a personality profile such as the Myers Briggs test or DISC assessment, and explore the significance of your natural style.
- Read *The Gifts of Imperfection: Let Go of Who You Think You're Supposed to Be and Embrace Who You Are* by Brené Brown (Hazelden, 2010).

Chapter 19

ॐ

Goddesses, Genesis, Guilt and Gold

UNHELPFUL PERSONALITY TRAITS are not the only way we can frustrate ourselves in the quest for soul enrichment. Another potential obstacle is a disconnect between our core values or belief system, and our day-to-day lives. If we are living at odds with what we actually believe about ourselves, our purpose and our work, then we might be preventing ourselves from experiencing the satisfaction that comes from a centred life.

Reflecting on four questions can help us identify the underlying principles that guide our thinking. These questions expose the basic paradigms that underpin our views of the world in four key areas:

1. how we view ourselves and our connections with others
2. how we view work and its role in our lives
3. how we handle the guilt that sometimes unsettles us
4. how we allow various aspects of life to preoccupy us in unhealthy ways.

Question 1: Am I a goddess?

All of us have particular views of ourselves. "Who am I?" is one of the most fundamental human questions. How we see ourselves, and how we see others in relation to ourselves, can easily affect our sense of soul enrichment.

If we listen carefully to the messages around us, we will hear lots of versions of who we are:

- We are a bunch of molecules collected randomly for no particular purpose.
- We are economic pawns being manipulated by gigantic economic forces and global injustice.
- We are created by a good and loving God to live, love and serve with meaning.
- We are created by a vindictive and unpredictable God for entertainment value.
- We are a community divided by gender and race, where oppression of one another cripples our ability to function freely.
- We are reincarnated beings who are constrained by our past wrongdoings.
- We are inherently flawed and capable of great evil.
- We are inherently good and capable of wonderful things.
- We are evolved beings created by time and chance seeking to pass on our genes to the next generation.

For me it is the Judeo-Christian explanation that most makes sense of who I am and explains the mixture of good and bad I see in myself and others. It suggests we were created to be good, but by turning our backs on our inherent purpose we ended up having a great capacity for evil. When we look around at the world, we see this is often so. Some people strive for and achieve awesome things; others inflict cruel and unjust pain on those around them.

At university I was told I was a goddess and should tap in to the "power within". I could do anything I wanted to, and I could do it single-handed. Nonsense! Whilst I support the power of positive thinking, I am not an advocate of positive self-delusion. Truth beats imagination. Reality beats delusion.

I am not a goddess. I cannot do everything myself. And acting as if I can is a great recipe for stress and disappointment.

The fundamental principles of Alcoholics Anonymous are, firstly, to admit we can't help ourselves and, secondly, to reach out to another stronger power. The fact is that we cannot do it alone. I don't believe we can handle how we use our time or how we nurture our souls without some outside help – through family, loved ones, soul sisters, community, church and especially our creator God. In fact, for some unfortunate people who end up socially isolated or ostracised by others, their only source of outside help may be God.

It is worth considering if our views about ourselves and whether we can thrive without outside help are assisting with our soul enrichment or undermining it. Valerie Volk has explored our need for others in her poem *One Hand*.[90]

One Hand

The sound of one hand clapping

First time I heard that line
I laughed.
The sheer absurdity
was somehow humorous,
almost touching.

But then my smiling died.
So sad.
One hand alone
unable to show anyone
how much it valued
what it had been given;
how much approved
all that it had been shown.

So much alone,
so separated
from the world of sharing.

Single-handed.

Should we admire this
(often quite self-satisfied)
assertion of achievement?

Alone.
Another word that sounds a knell,
reminding us that
if we spurn the place
of others in our lives
we are diminished.

Alone, we fall...
silently.

But one hand can reach out.

Valerie Volk (2014).

Question 2: Does my world view affect the way I work?

Stephanie's father was an A-type driven entrepreneur who influenced her to become a highly driven and successful professional – until in her early 40s she hit a wall, lost her marriage, lost her job and almost lost her identity. (Chapter 13 tells Stephanie's story.) For many like Steph, work provides their identity, their meaning and their reason for being.

We often inherit our attitude towards work. For some, work is the means by which to rise to the top and make the most money. For others, work is an inconvenient necessity to be avoided if possible.

There are some for whom work is all about productivity and seasons. My father was a farmer. As a child I saw him spend all day and night on the tractor when making sure the seed was in the ground before the rains came. I always understood there were times and seasons to work hard (sometimes very hard) and then there was a time to play on the beach.

For still others, work is all toil and labour – a pointless chore that is never satisfying. Of course, we should not be surprised that life is pretty tough at times. According to *Genesis* (the biblical book, not the musical group!), there will always be sweat and toil associated with making a living.[91] On the farm it became pretty obvious that just because you worked hard to put in the seed did not mean the rains would come and the harvest would be plentiful. There are droughts and famines and court cases and bankruptcies. There are threats to health and other crises plainly beyond our control.

Again, when it comes to work, the Judeo-Christian approach makes sense of things for me. It explains that we are all created to be productive and to work for the good of ourselves, each other and the world around us. Work is inherently good and gives us purpose and dignity. However, because we are all disconnected from our creator, our work has become laborious toil. Work is regularly frustrating and hard.

However, our creator never abandons us to our messy lives, but joins us in the mess and personally restores us. Work too can be restorative and contribute to glimpses of what a life well-lived can be. Our work can enrich others, bless us and contribute positively to the world we live in.

There is little benefit in seeing work as the core source of our worth and identity. That is destined to one day disappoint. Nor is work just a necessary evil for making a living. That view is just soul destroying.

It is useful to identify the attitude we have towards work, and the elements and origin of our world view. The following poem *I Am a Woman* (which is best read aloud with a friend, with one voice for the factory owner's wife and one voice for the peasant woman) shows the stark reality that divides two very different perspectives on the world. Sometimes we inadvertently live and work in a manner that is opposed to the views we actually hold, and so we create an obstacle to our soul enrichment.

This poem is attributed to a working class Chilean woman, who is reported to have written it in 1973 shortly after the overthrow of Chile's socialist president, Salvador Allende, through a military coup led by Augusto Pinochet. An American missionary is said to have translated the poem and taken it home to the United States when she was forced to leave Chile.

I Am a Woman

I am a woman.
I am a woman.

I am a woman born of a woman whose man owned a factory.
I am a woman born of a woman whose man laboured in a factory.

I am a woman whose man wore silk suits, who constantly watched his weight.
I am a woman whose man wore tattered clothing, whose heart was constantly strangled by hunger.

I am a woman who watched two babies grow into beautiful children.
I am a woman who watched two babies die because there was no milk.

I am a woman who watched twins grow into popular college students with summers abroad.
I am a woman who watched three children grow, but with bellies stretched from no food.

But then there was a man;
But then there was a man;

And he talked about the peasants getting richer by my family getting poorer.
And he told me of days that would be better and he made the days better.

We had to eat rice.
We had rice.

We had to eat beans!
We had beans.

My children were no longer given summer visas to Europe.
My children no longer cried themselves to sleep.

And I felt like a peasant.
And I felt like a woman.

A peasant with a dull, hard, unexciting life.
Like a woman with a life that sometimes allowed a song.

And I saw a man.
And I saw a man.

And together we began to plot with the hope of the return to freedom.
I saw his heart begin to beat with hope of freedom, at last.

Someday, the return to freedom.
Someday freedom.

And then,
But then,

One day,
One day,

There were planes overhead and guns firing close by.
There were planes overhead and guns firing in the distance.

I gathered my children and went home.
I gathered my children and ran.

And the guns moved farther and farther away.
But the guns moved closer and closer.

And then, they announced that freedom had been restored!
And then they came, young boys really.

They came into my home along with my man.
They came and found my man.

Those men whose money was almost gone.
They found all of the men whose lives were almost their own.

And we all had drinks to celebrate.
And they shot them all.

The most wonderful martinis.
They shot my man.

And then they asked us to dance.
And they came for me.

Me.
For me, the woman.

And my sisters.
For my sisters.

And then they took us.
Then they took us.

They took us to dinner at a small private club.
They stripped from us the dignity we had gained.

And they treated us to beef.
And then they raped us.

It was one course after another.
One after another they came after us.

We nearly burst we were so full.
Lunging, plunging – sisters bleeding, sisters dying.

It was magnificent to be free again!
It was hardly a relief to have survived.

The beans have almost disappeared now.
The beans have disappeared.

The rice – I've replaced it with chicken or steak.
The rice, I cannot find it.

**And the parties continue night after night to make up for all
the time wasted.**
And my silent tears are joined once more by the midnight cries
of my children.

And I feel like a woman again.
They say, I am a woman.

Attributed to a working class Chilean woman (1973).

Question 3: Should I feel guilty for working?

Guilt is a funny thing these days. It has almost become one of those dirty words: never let yourself feel guilty, they tell us; have no regrets. But once upon a time, guilt and regret were respected as accurate responses of a well-honed conscience.

Many voices speak to us about the appropriate level of guilt to experience. I used to believe that my university academic career was more "worthy" than the commercial recruitment job that followed it, until the CEO of a huge corporation rolled his eyes at me and suggested the exact opposite. He hinted that an academic vocation was not a "real job" and that the world of business was more valuable. (I have actually loved both vocations.) Another friend suggested that the only worthy profession was to work for a "not for profit" organisation. I know of a woman who impressed on her children that the best professions were those providing service in medicine, education and similar industries. Of course, the "green movement" condemns logging as a profession, vegetarians call butchers' shops into question and plenty of people condemn workers in the nuclear or tobacco industries.

Guilt may be the result of living inconsistently with our own values. Our beliefs might be to value children and family over work; to value the environment over destructive mining and logging practices; or to value people over profit and honesty over lies. If we have fallen into a job that is at odds with these values, then any resulting guilt could be best described as a healthy functioning conscience.

It is also easy to feel guilty if you and your loved ones are not thriving because of your work commitments. Children and partners, parents and friends can all feel neglected when our priorities are focussed elsewhere. So taking an honest and healthy look at ourselves and our relationships is important if we don't want to lose what is most precious to us. A good first step is to ask: am I in the right place or should there be a change? Alternatively, would both I and my loved ones suffer more if I were not working? Let's face it, most people have to earn a living.

If there are relationships that are more important to you than the extra money in your pay packet, many will tell you that you should take a part-time position or seek more flexible hours. Not following this kind of suggestion, with its subtle implication that working full-time necessarily means you are neglecting important relationships, can create a feeling of guilt.

Yet even as I write this, I am conscious that rarely will this advice be given to a man. Men have traditionally been honoured for their "breadwinning" role and less often criticised for the fact they are not completely there for the children. Annabel Crabb has highlighted research in her recent book *The Wife Drought* which shows that men who have children are positively facilitated in their careers while the opposite is true for women. Women who have children are perceived as less reliable and less attractive as employees and managers.[92] Annabel argues that just as women have been encouraged to engage more fully in the public sphere, so men need to be given encouragement to engage more fully in the domestic sphere.[93]

The question of guilt is explored poignantly in the folk-rock song *Cat's in the Cradle*. This song tells of a son who grows up and neglects his aging father – just as his father neglected him as a child. So sometimes our twinge of guilt is simply our healthy conscience telling us we are out of kilter.

But there are also times when our guilt is unwarranted self-chastisement, because we are actually doing the best we can in the circumstances we've been given. Or sometimes we feel guilty for no other reason than that people project guilt onto us. One nice church-going lady once suggested to me that I should be careful not to get too successful in my work as I might be getting out of step with my husband. At the time I did not actually have a husband!

Our social context can also affect our sense of guilt. When I was at university 30 years ago, an important community for me was my church; but there were few women there who were able to guide me in relation to starting my career as a lawyer or an educator. Instead, there seemed to be an inordinate amount of emphasis on craft workshops and preparation for child rearing duties. Given I have never really enjoyed crafts and have not had any babies (despite plans to the contrary), I could easily have been tempted to feel guilty for not conforming to the picture of a "good Christian woman". However, that really would have been self-inflicted guilt.

Fortunately, my current experience of church has been quite different. There are now far more female mentors to guide young professionals, and the idea that "a woman's place is in the home" seems long abandoned. After all, the last chapter of the biblical *Book of Proverbs* shows that a "good wife" (or "good woman") is one who runs an array of businesses in a commercial and profitable manner.[94] It is also evident from the Bible's account in *Genesis* that Adam and Eve were *together* created by God to work.[95]

This is not to suggest that mothers are not working. And according to one professional friend of mine, giving birth to children was actually the hardest and most painful work of all. Unfortunately, the rising numbers of women in the workforce creates its own new version of guilt – the self-imposed guilt of superwoman envy!

So make sure you identify where your guilt is coming from. Is it emanating from a life out of kilter and a good functioning conscience? Or is it unwarranted self-criticism or the creation of ill-founded finger-pointing by well-meaning friends? Some good old-fashioned soul searching should help us determine the source of our guilt, and stop it from becoming an unnecessary obstacle to the enrichment of our souls.

Cat's in the Cradle

My child arrived just the other day,
He came to the world in the usual way.
But there were planes to catch, and bills to pay.
He learned to walk while I was away.
And he was talking 'fore I knew it, and as he grew,
He'd say, "I'm gonna be like you, Dad.
You know I'm gonna be like you."

And the cat's in the cradle and the silver spoon,
Little boy blue and the man in the moon.
"When you coming home, Dad?" "I don't know when,
But we'll get together then.
You know we'll have a good time then."

My son turned ten just the other day.
He said, "Thanks for the ball, Dad, come on let's play.
Can you teach me to throw?" I said, "Not today,
I got a lot to do." He said, "That's OK."
And he walked away, but his smile never dimmed,
Said, "I'm gonna be like him, yeah.
You know I'm gonna be like him."

And the cat's in the cradle and the silver spoon,
Little boy blue and the man in the moon.
"When you coming home, Dad?" "I don't know when,
But we'll get together then.
You know we'll have a good time then."

Well, he came from college just the other day,
So much like a man I just had to say,
"Son, I'm proud of you. Can you sit for a while?"
He shook his head, and he said with a smile,
"What I'd really like, Dad, is to borrow the car keys.
See you later. Can I have them please?"

And the cat's in the cradle and the silver spoon,
Little boy blue and the man in the moon.
"When you coming home, son?" "I don't know when,
But we'll get together then, Dad.
You know we'll have a good time then."

I've long since retired and my son's moved away.
I called him up just the other day.
I said, "I'd like to see you if you don't mind."
He said, "I'd love to, Dad, if I could find the time.

You see, my new job's a hassle, and the kid's got the flu,
But it's sure nice talking to you, Dad.
It's been sure nice talking to you."

And as I hung up the phone, it occurred to me,
He'd grown up just like me.
My boy was just like me.

And the cat's in the cradle and the silver spoon,
Little boy blue and the man in the moon.
"When you coming home, son?" "I don't know when,
But we'll get together then, Dad.
You know we'll have a good time then."

Based on a poem written by Sandra Campbell Chapin, and later adapted
for music by her husband, Harry Chapin (from the album 'Verities &
Balderdash', 1974).

Question 4: What have my idols got to do with it?

Liang and her husband were wealthy, successful and made the perfect
couple. But she remembers walking home to their harbour-side
apartment one night after being promoted by her investment bank
to the coveted senior manager level, and she was surprised to find
herself despairing because of the emptiness she felt. She "had it all",
but it was if she had nothing. She couldn't understand why reaching
all of her targets had not warmed her heart. It seemed that Liang had
been aiming for certain goals which did not actually satisfy her soul.
(Chapter 10 tells Liang's story.)

As she looked around her, Liang could also see how many of her
peers were discontented. One of her colleagues was addicted to Chanel,
Escada and Prada. She was well known for spending $2000 or $3000
on a single suit of clothes for work. And she commonly spent between
$3000 and $5000 on designer handbags. She changed her handbags
daily and was rarely seen wearing the same outfit twice. Her addiction
meant her expensive shopping outings happened at least fortnightly.

She confided in Liang that the "happiness and contentment" she received with each purchase sadly only lasted about a week, by which time she began searching for her next purchase. She admitted that in the end her fortnightly shopping expeditions were just reinforcing an emptiness inside.

So what is an idol? It's the thing that fills our mind, the thing we value above all else and the thing we make sacrifices for. However, it is not going to provide the fulfilment we crave.

It is often claimed that the most crippling idols are *money, sex* and *power*. It is not surprising that when one of these idols controls our life and work, there are serious casualties. Making money by working incredibly long hours is a cultural imperative in Singapore – so much so that apparently the government has now taken to erecting signs in railway stations to remind people that family is also an important aspect of life. It is commonly said in some cultures for a man to become the President of the country, there is a prerequisite to have a mistress – how else can a man show his potency? And power takes pride of place in most countries' political circles – with the temptation of corruption following not far behind.

The same three seductions are also referred to as *gold, girls* and *glory*. Not surprisingly, most women find this description hard to relate to, so I have formulated a new list that I've found more often rings true for professional women. We can end up being enslaved by *possessions, passion* and *position*.

Consider this in the light of the popular TV series *Sex and the City*. Carrie collected Manolo Blahnik shoes (usually worth over $1000 per pair); Samantha was addicted to sex; Miranda was obsessed with her career; and Charlotte was consumed with making the right marriage. What fascinated me about the whole show was that the finale ended up being nothing about sex and all about "love".

Carrie finally found love with Mr Big; Samantha's libido vanished due to her chemotherapy for breast cancer, but she was heartened when her boyfriend Smith told her he loved her anyway; Miranda and her husband decided that love would be the thing to get them through the dilemmas of caring for his mother who had dementia; and

Charlotte and her husband, Harry, were focussing all their love on a child they planned to adopt. This television series showcased all of the main obsessions of our current era, and yet it finally found those idols wanting. In the end it belied its name and returned to a soul enriching focus on love.

The problem with idols is that they become obsessions that never fully satisfy us. The famous sonnet *Ozymandias* by Shelley is a startling reminder of the frailty of the idols which can seem so powerful when they take centre stage.

My mother taught me something very sensible when I was a child. She said we can all make good or bad choices, but if we choose the "bad" too often, then we tend to lose the power to choose. The "bad choice" starts to choose us. It's as if making too many bad choices results in dulling our conscience and makes us see things very dimly. In his famous "sermon on the mount" Jesus said, "For where your treasure is, there your heart will be also."[96]

There is an old Cherokee Indian legend in which a grandfather teaches his grandson about the terrible fight between the two wolves inside all of us – the evil wolf and the good wolf. When the boy asks which will win, the grandfather tells him: "The one you feed." If the obstacle to your soul enrichment is an unhealthy preoccupation with an idol in your life, then you might just have to stop feeding that wolf. Alternatively, you might need to call on friends for an intervention.

Finally, putting into practice some of the 60 second solutions and other remedies in this book may help to lift you out of a particular rut, or to bring some inspiration to a soul in survival mode. Once you kick that idol out of your heart, you free up all sorts of room for more joy and soul enrichment.

Ozymandias

I met a traveller from an antique land
Who said: "Two vast and trunkless legs of stone
Stand in the desert. Near them, on the sand,
Half sunk, a shattered visage lies, whose frown,

And wrinkled lip, and sneer of cold command,
Tell that its sculptor well those passions read
Which yet survive, stamped on these lifeless things,
The hand that mocked them and the heart that fed:
And on the pedestal these words appear:
'My name is Ozymandias, king of kings:
Look on my works, ye Mighty, and despair!'
Nothing beside remains. Round the decay
Of that colossal wreck, boundless and bare
The lone and level sands stretch far away".

A sonnet by Percy Bysshe Shelley, published in The Examiner in London (11 January 1818).

Chapter 20

କ୍ଷ

Redundancy and Other Dirty Words

REDUNDANCY, SICKNESS, resignation, termination, injustice, politics, injury, discrimination, retirement and other inescapable circumstances can result in us suddenly being outside of paid work. What happens when our discretionary time is dramatically increased but we feel completely miserable?

There is nothing like the cessation of our daily employment to remind us how soul enriching we found our work. On the other hand, perhaps we have landed in a job that is soul destroying, and we desperately wish we could return to something more rewarding.

Nancy Wake experienced this on a grand scale when the Second World War ended. Nancy is one of Australia's most decorated WWII heroes (she was born in New Zealand but grew up in Sydney). Operating as both a British agent and a leader in the French Resistance, she was one of the Nazis' most wanted opponents. They dubbed her the White Mouse because she always seemed to slip away and escape capture.

When the war ended, Nancy felt at a loose end. She had thrived during her four years with the French Resistance, and the boredom of being back in the normal world was excruciating. She found it hard to shake off the restlessness of no longer being in the thick of the battle, and despite having all the time in the world, life was just not satisfying for her.[97] Eventually she decided to run for parliament in Australia, which provided her with a new battle to fight.

So what is going on when we are suddenly rich in time and our inner well-being plummets into free-fall? This is a good time to recognise that richness of soul can have little to do with discretionary time and more to do with our response to the cards that life deals us. Are we going to stay dissatisfied, angry, depressed or bitter about our new under-employed status? Or can we redirect our emotional energy into taking advantage of the break that is being forced upon us?

It is natural to be distressed if misfortune intervenes in our career, but sometimes the obstacle to soul enrichment is getting stuck in that distress and not being able to move on.

One way to progress is to take advantage of our extra discretionary time and invest in activities that promote soul enrichment and well-being. It is an opportunity to be intentional about what we focus on. Of course, we may have very little spare time if every day is consumed with looking for a new job, or recovering from the illness or injury that brought our work to an end. In that case, we may need to return to 60 second solutions!

Stephanie

When Stephanie lost her job because of a forced redundancy she was immediately shocked and numb. She had been working ridiculously long hours for the company and was excellent at her job. The redundancy came out of the blue. For the first few weeks she was in a state of denial, feeling as if she was just on holiday leave. However, the reality soon set in that her high profile and satisfying job had disappeared into thin air.

Chapter 13 describes how at one point Steph had made a desperate plea to the heavens that if there was a God up there, she would like to see a sign. Ironically, her redundancy was announced almost straight after that prayer. It was not the sign she was hoping for. However, rather than dwell on her loss, Steph took the opportunity to spend more time with friends. It was not long before she was very grateful for the forced break. Over the following few weeks she started to explore Christianity, and she is now convinced she needed to take time out from her frenetic work schedule to stop long enough to find God (or to let God find her, as she likes to say).

I am not suggesting that everyone whose job is made redundant is going to find God! However, there is a freedom in using the newfound space to pursue something you find soul enriching. If you have always wanted to do a painting course, this is the moment to sign up. If you have always wanted to learn ballroom dancing, it is definitely time to buy your dancing shoes. If you have always wanted to take a trip to Africa to dig a well or help in an orphanage, it is time to book your ticket.

Anne

When I was 23 I was in a terrible car accident and my neck was broken in three places. I had only been out of university for one year, and I was about to start a new job as a high school teacher in regional South Australia. The school held my position while I spent a few weeks in the Royal Adelaide Hospital's spinal unit, and many more weeks in a metal brace, waiting for the bones to knit back together. I was off work for a whole semester.

I did not know you could break your neck and not die. I was lucky because the car landed upside down. I was unconscious, and my hair was caught through the broken window and under the roof of the car. It was as if I was in traction. My C2 vertebrae had a "hangman's fracture", which is where the bones are broken all the way through. My spinal cord was unsupported, so if the car had landed on its wheels, I would have either died or become a quadriplegic from the impact of my head slumping forward. But somehow I survived.

Despite all of this, my circumstances paled into insignificance in the light of the fact that one of my friends died in that car accident. I found myself crying at the most unexpected moments every day for the next year – always thinking of my friend's life cut short, and of his family and friends who were devastated by the loss of this beautiful man. No platitudes from my friends or reminders that it was an "accident" could make this situation OK. Death is a decisive sadness, and it will usually cause unspeakable pain.

During that semester of recovery, I did a lot of thinking about life and death. It was the first time I had really appreciated that every day is a gift, and we cannot know when our time will come to an end.

So how does your soul survive when the pain of life is overwhelming and you are losing the fight against anger, depression or sadness? My experience was not that "things were made better"; rather, I was sustained by the fact I was not alone in the sadness. My friends and family were kind and present – a regular stream of visitors came to my bed. And surprisingly, the fiery presence of God was tangibly real to me.

I had grown up in a Christian home, but I never assumed that being a Christian exempted me from pain. I just believed that God could be trusted, even in the most difficult times. So when I woke up in that mangled car wreck, one of my first thoughts was: "God is bigger than all of this, and he is here." It is hard to describe how strange it was to be lying in a hospital spinal unit unable to move and sad beyond words, and yet to be comforted by a sense of God's presence.

So when we are suddenly not working, it is useful to protect our souls by being mindful about the way we use our newly acquired discretionary time. And in the worst case scenario, when pursuing soul enrichment seems impossible, we should remember we are not alone, and look for the soul food that can be brought to us by others who are standing by ready to share our burdens.

One Morning *(the morning after Australia Day, 1988)*

Mangled mass of metal
Tight
Jagged brittle
I am breathing
Dirt air voices

My neck hurts
It's all right dear – we'll get you out
Oh my God
Don't move now – you'll be OK
Oh Lord, no
The others...are they all right?
...Yes dear – we'll have you out soon
Who...who was driving?
You were dear
Oh my God

Chapter 21

༄

Stillness and Other Healing Words

I WILL HAVE FAILED if you have reached this final chapter and you feel burdened by a new layer of obligations. There is nothing soul enriching about trying to discharge a list of soul enriching duties! Also, you may have tried many of the suggestions in this book but still crave an inner peace that eludes you.

It may be that a key obstacle to your soul enrichment has less to do with your day-to-day behaviour and more to do with a far deeper question.

Angelica

Angelica started her first business when she was just four years old. She grew up with her grandmother in the Philippines, and for her fourth birthday her grandmother gave her some money so she could buy a scooter. Angelica worked out she could charge the local kids 20 cents for a five-minute ride on her scooter, and after carefully settling her customer list, she launched her small business in the local area. When she had collected quite a bit of money, she asked her grandmother to help her buy a second scooter. By the time she was five years old, she had four scooters, a thriving local business and a loan she was paying off to her grandmother.

Angelica developed a feisty backbone at a very early age, and since then she has always been driven to succeed. When she was still a child, she and some young aunties were kidnapped on their way home from a party. Four men hijacked them in a jeepney, and it was six-year-old Angelica who aggressively negotiated with the armed men to take the girls home in return for money and jewellery. She insisted that the kidnappers be true to their word, and it worked. The girls were returned home.

At the age of 11, Angelica migrated to Australia with her family, and she learned to stand up to the succession of sleazy men who regularly asked her if she was a Filipino bride married to an older man. Angelica describes her early decades as being fuelled by adrenaline, gumption and a lot of anger. Despite the objections of her father, she left home at 15 with $50 in her pocket to sell Encyclopaedia Britannicas.

In her late 20s, Angelica resolved that she wanted to make $2 million and retire by the age of 45. When she was 38 she had accumulated $1.9 million worth of houses and other assets (including an eight-bedroom mansion outside Perth). However, soon after reaching her goal she lost it all. She lost the mansion through a bad business decision, and over the next couple of years, all of her other accumulated wealth and houses disappeared. Her investments failed, her marriage failed and she lost her identity. The fight had gone from her.

It was then that she wondered if God could make any difference to her life.

Angelica had grown up in the Catholic tradition in the Philippines, but despite believing in God and the idea that Jesus was her saviour, she still had many niggling questions. She was not clear about how to get to heaven, and she kept searching for truth about God in a variety of places, including in Hinduism, Buddhism, a local church cult, the Jehovah's Witnesses and various Protestant denominations including Churches of Christ, Presbyterian, Uniting, Anglican and Pentecostal churches.

In her search for satisfaction, Angelica also tried interior designing, painting, poetry writing, community service, volunteer work, women in motorsports, yachting and learning to fly. Basically she dipped into most of the areas of life that I suggest can be easily neglected when we are busy. She tried generosity to abused women; she embraced adversity; she facilitated vitality through numerous sporting endeavours; she indulged in creativity; and she dabbled in all sorts of spiritual pursuits. But still nothing satisfied her.

Now nearly ten years later Angelica says she is a new person. She says she feels peace and inner joy that nothing in her life had previously provided. She feels an inner strength that none of her own gumption or feistiness could achieve. And she puts it all down to being still, surrendering to God and finding out what it really meant to let God love and restore her.

As a good Catholic girl, Angelica knew intellectually that God was supposed to love her. But she could not understand what that meant, nor feel what it was like. All she knew were moral obligations. When her business and personal life went into free-fall, Angelica decided to stop and try something different. She started to talk to God, usually sticking to simple prayers such as "OK, I am here", "I don't know what I am looking for" and "I don't know what to do."

Then Angelica slowly started making changes in her life. Until a few years ago, she always worked a 12-day fortnight, including on the one weekend each fortnight when her twin boys were with their father. Now she rarely works on a Sunday. At first this was not to go to church but just to stop and be still. She also sought out some wise counsel by joining a leadership group with other like-minded business people.

Now Angelica says she has changed. Instead of being desperate to always succeed (and trying valiantly to avoid God's gaze), Angelica says she can look God in the eye because God's love and forgiveness are very real to her. Angelica feels an internal joy and serenity that she says is not affected by her circumstances. She says she can survive a storm or a desert experience because she knows the love and presence of God. She now has her anger under control (instead of it controlling her), and her friends also say she is not as judgmental and critical as she used to be, and is quieter in her soul.

For Angelica, soul enrichment ultimately came from working out what it meant that God loved her, not from succeeding in the long list of her own endeavours. When all else fails, be still – ask for help – and keep watch in case an answer is right there waiting to love you.

Appendix

&

Time Audit Survey

IF YOU ARE UNCERTAIN whether or not you have any discretionary time, you can do a quick review by completing the following time audit chart. Consider a "typical week" in your life, and record three types of activities in three different colours:

1. unchanging obligations (such as delivering children to school or travelling to work)
2. variable obligations (such as meal times)
3. discretionary and unallocated time (such as watching TV or relaxing).

Activities may include sleeping, ablutions, travelling, working, cooking, eating, meetings, attendance at events, childcare, shopping, study, sports, recreation, volunteer work, etc. Calculate the total minutes of discretionary time you have in a week by writing the total at the bottom of each day.

Daily time	Mon. activity	Tues. activity	Wed. activity	Thurs. activity	Fri. activity	Sat. activity	Sun. activity
12.00 midnight							
1.00am							
2.00am							
3.00am							
4.00am							
5.00am							
6.00am							
7.00am							
8.00am							
9.00am							
10.00am							
11.00am							
12.00 midday							

Daily time	Mon. activity	Tues. activity	Wed. activity	Thurs. activity	Fri. activity	Sat. activity	Sun. activity
1.00pm							
2.00pm							
3.00pm							
4.00pm							
5.00pm							
6.00pm							
7.00pm							
8.00pm							
9.00pm							
10.00pm							
11.00pm							

Total time that is discretionary:

You may also like to consider whether or not you have longer periods of discretionary time at different points in the year (for instance, on public holidays and when you take annual leave from work). Record in this chart any free days you can foresee:

Month	Week 1	Week 2	Week 3	Week 4	Week 5
January					
February					
March					
April					
May					
June					
July					
August					
September					
October					
November					
December					

You may find it interesting to compare your typical daily time usage to some of the recent average scenarios provided by research in the USA and Australia. Research in 2013 by the American Bureau of Labor Statistics concluded that the following "time use" applied to an average work day for employed persons aged 25 to 54 with children under 18 (with each category including travel time):

Working and related activities	8.7 hours
Sleeping	7.7 hours
Leisure and sports	2.5 hours
Caring for others	1.3 hours
Household activities	1.1 hours
Eating and drinking	1.0 hours
Other	1.7 hours

It is worth noting that working women with children under six (as opposed to men) had slightly higher statistics for "caring for others" (1.9 hours) and "household activities" (1.3 hours); whereas their "working and related activities" took less time (7.7 hours), as did their "leisure and sports" (2.1 hours).[98]

In 2006 the Australian Bureau of Statistics published a report on *How Australians Use Their Time*.[99] Some of the enlightening findings for women (not necessarily women in paid work) were as follows:

Recreation and leisure	16% of their day (3 hours 57 minutes)	Compared with 19% for men
Domestic activities	12% of their day (2 hours 52 minutes)	Compared with 7% for men

Afterword & Acknowledgments

❧

How Did I Write This Book?

GIVEN I CLAIM TO BE TIME-POOR, it is reasonable to ask how I ever managed to write this book. Well, it is quite clear I could not have done it without the help of my friends, without the discipline of prioritising the project over other responsibilities that had to be put aside for a time and, most importantly, without some divine intervention! Also, the project was certainly helped by the fact that I've always loved writing, and that constructing clarity out of chaos and writing about it is one of the creative outlets that gives me joy and enriches my soul.

For those who love practical guidelines, here is a summary of how I went about writing this book:

1. I have had a passion for the topic for years.
2. I had a goal or vision to write the book many years ago.
3. I kept a folder full of ideas as I thought about the issues and did the odd bit of research.
4. I took a weekend out each year to go on a personal retreat, to reflect and pray about the year past and the year to come, and to formulate some key priorities for the year ahead.
5. I finally decided it was time to actually put pen to paper.
6. I resigned from being the convenor of a professional women's organisation to make more time in my crammed life in order to prioritise the project.

7. I gave myself a target date for completion (12 months), which I confess had to be almost doubled in the end.
8. I wrote an outline of the book, which became a draft table of contents.
9. I collected a group of friends who were willing to support me, keep me accountable and pray for me; and I wrote emails every month or two with an account of my progress and a list of areas where I asked for their prayers.
10. I collected another group who were willing to read my draft chapters and give me constructive feedback.
11. I attended a writing group with two of my friends, and we met erratically to critique each other's work.
12. I came to an understanding between me and God that I would sit down to write for two hours each Saturday at 2.00pm, and if that time was not available, then at 4.00pm, and again on Sunday afternoon if Saturday proved impossible.
13. I found a comfortable, quiet place in my house where I could set up my laptop and be undisturbed when I was writing.
14. I sought wisdom from the Bible and asked for help from God before most attempts to write.
15. I had a weekly writing goal, where I was attempting to complete a certain section each week.
16. I organised ahead the various interviews with professional women in order to give impetus for writing my case studies.
17. I sometimes focussed on the "fun" parts of the project (such as finding the right photos to illustrate the book) to give myself added motivation.
18. I created an improvised front cover to assist with imagining what the finished product might look like (and to inspire me to actually complete the project).
19. I imagined what a website might look like to promote the published book.
20. I regularly printed and bound the draft book to easily carry it around and proofread it when possible, such as when I was on the train or in a boring seminar.

In a nutshell, I could not have completed this project without a passion for the topic, creative ideas and self-discipline – all of which I give God the credit for. I am also completely indebted to the many friends who supported me and gave me invaluable feedback on the book, and to the many women who shared their stories with me, knowing that their vulnerabilities would be shared with the world at large. Thank you to you all – you know who you are!

Finally, I am also blessed with the gift of a tolerant, patient, kind and encouraging husband whom I adore. Thank you John. And we must not forget my cute little white dog, who regularly took up his position at my feet to keep me company as I wrote. Bless you Billy.

Endnotes

1. Arianna Huffington, *Thrive: The Third Metric to Redefining Success and Creating a Happier Life*, WH Allen, 2014, p. 255.
2. Jean-Jacques Rousseau, French political philosopher, novelist, author and composer; from the translation by Barbara Foxley of *Emile*, 1762, Book IV.
3. Not as many of us may be aware that this quote is attributed to Jesus in the biblical book of the *Acts of the Apostles* 20:35.
4. King Solomon, son of King David and Bathsheba, King of Israel (c. 970–931 BC); from the *Book of Proverbs* 11:25 (NKJV translation of the Bible).
5. Anne Manne, *The Life of I: The New Culture of Narcissism*, Melbourne University Press, 2014, p. 204.
6. Anne Manne, p. 204.
7. Maya Angelou (1928–2014), African-American poet, author, journalist, singer, actor, film maker, civil rights activist and university professor.
8. Arianna Huffington, *Thrive*, p. 4.
9. C.S. Lewis, ex-atheist, writer, academic, medievalist and Christian theologian; from *The Four Loves*, Fontana Books, 1963, p. 7.
10. An ancient Jewish teacher; from the *Book of Ecclesiastes* 4:9–12 (NRSV translation of the Bible).
11. John T. Cacioppo & William Patrick, *Loneliness: Human Nature and the Need for Social Connection*, W.W. Norton & Co., 2008, p. 93.
12. Linda Grayson, American product designer, giftware producer, decorative artist and owner of Printwick Papers.
13. Helen Keller, American deaf and blind writer and political activist, communicated in the 1920s in response to the question "Do you desire your sight more than anything else in the world?"; from Joseph P. Lash, *Helen and Teacher: The Story of Helen Keller and Anne Sullivan Macy*, Perseus Publishing, 1980, p. 498.
14. Stephen Marche, "Is Facebook Making Us Lonely?" *The Atlantic*, 2 April 2012.
15. Suzanne Goldsmith, American author; from *A City Year: On the Streets and in the Neighborhoods with Twelve Young Community Service Volunteers*, Transaction Publishers, 1998, p. 277.
16. Desmond Tutu, South African Anglican bishop, human rights activist, opponent of apartheid and winner of numerous peace prizes; from *God Is Not a Christian: And Other Provocations*, HarperCollins, 2011, p. 50.
17. Israelmore Ayivor, motivational speaker and writer from Ghana, registered nurse and Christian youth leader; from his website, http://israelmoreayivor.com/2014/06/09/.

18. Jesus (c. 4 BC–30 AD), born in Bethlehem; son of Mary and Joseph, Jewish Rabbi and founder of Christianity; from the account of Jesus' life written by his disciple Matthew, *Matthew* 5:9 (NIV translation of the Bible).
19. Desmond Tutu, *God Is Not a Christian*, p. 24.
20. Gordon Neufeld, Canadian psychologist, expert on child development and attachment theory; from "Holding on to Your Kids in a Digital Age: An Interview with Gordon Neufeld, Part 2", Omega Institute for Holistic Studies, posted on 29 March 2013, www.eomega.org/learning-paths/relationships-family-family/gordon-neufeld-sil-reynolds-holding-on-to-your-kids-in-a-digital-age.
21. Cate Blanchett, Australian actor, theatre artistic director, champion of eco-sustainability; from an interview with Leslie Bennetts, "A Hollywood Elusive", *Vanity Fair*, February 2009.
22. Ken Costa is reported to have said that the greatest casualty of a busy life is "intimacy with God", in Mark Greene, *Supporting Christians at Work (Without Going Insane)*, Administry and LICC, 2001, p. 12.
23. Brad Meltzer, American novelist, comic book writer and TV show creator; from his novel *The Inner Circle*, Hodder & Stoughton, 2011, p. 331.
24. King Solomon, *Book of Proverbs* 18:24 (GWT translation of the Bible).
25. Brené Brown, *Daring Greatly: How the Courage to Be Vulnerable Transforms the Way We Live, Love, Parent and Lead*, Penguin Books, 2012, pp. 103–104.
26. Brené Brown, p. 104.
27. Elisabeth Kübler-Ross, Swiss-American psychiatrist and researcher into death and dying; from *Death: The Final Stage of Growth*, Touchstone, 1975, p. 93.
28. An ancient Jewish teacher, *Book of Ecclesiastes* 3:11 (NIV translation of the Bible).
29. Aleksandr Solzhenitsyn, Russian writer, historian and soldier; as translated by the members of the BBC Russian Service in *'One Word of Truth...' The Nobel Speech on Literature 1970*, The Bodley Head, 1972, p. 5.
30. Harriet Beecher Stowe, American abolitionist, novelist and writer; from *Uncle Tom's Cabin,* 1852, Belknap Press, 2009, chapter 13, p. 176.
31. John Keats, English Romantic poet; from his poem *Endymion*, 1818.
32. Sojourner Truth (born Isabella Baumfree), African-American woman, ex-slave, human rights activist, travelling preacher, spoken at the Women's Rights Convention in Akron, Ohio, May 1851, as recounted by Frances D. Gage, President of the Akron Convention; in Elizabeth Stanton, Susan Anthony & Matilda Gage (eds), *History of Woman Suffrage*, vol. 1, chapter 6, 1881, p. 116.

33. John Stuart Mill, 19th-century English philosopher, parliamentarian, atheist and political economist, home-schooled by his father and Jeremy Bentham; from his *Inaugural Address Delivered to the University of St. Andrews, Feb. 1st 1867*, Longmans, Green, Reader & Dyer, 1867, p. 36.
34. Quoted by Mr Scott of Georgia in his address to the US House of Representatives in the tribute "Remembering Rosa Parks" on 26 October 2005, *Congressional Record – House*, vol. 151, part 17, p. 23945. See also Rosa Parks with Jim Haskins, *Rosa Parks: My Story*, Puffin Books, 1992, p. 116.
35. Faith McDonnell & Grace Akallo, *Girl Soldier: A Story of Hope for Northern Uganda's Children*, Chosen Books, 2007, p. 123.
36. From the Austrian documentary film *Blind Spot – Hitler's Secretary*, directed by André Heller & Othmar Schmiderer, 2002.
37. As quoted in Johann Christoph Arnold, *Seeking Peace: Notes and Conversations Along the Way*, The Plough Publishing House, 2013, p. 154. See also Sophie Scholl's letter to Fritz Hartnagel, 22 June 1940 in *At the Heart of the White Rose: Letters and Diaries of Hans and Sophie Scholl*, Harper & Rowe, 1987, p. 75.
38. The Prophet Micah, born in a town in south-west Judah, written around 700 BC; from *Micah* 6:8, (NIV translation of the Bible).
39. Florence Nightingale, British nurse, social reformer, statistician, pioneer of modern nursing and the "Lady with the Lamp" during the Crimean War; "from her pen in 1896", quoted in Edward Tyas Cook, *The Life of Florence Nightingale*, vol. II, 1914, p. 406.
40. William Shakespeare, English playwright and poet; spoken by Brutus in *Julius Caesar*, 1599, Act 4, Scene 3.
41. Julie Andrews (born 1935), English actor, singer, dancer, entertainer and theatre director; from her website, www.julieandrewsonline.com/hightor.
42. King Solomon, *Book of Proverbs* 13:19 (NKJV translation of the Bible).
43. Helen Keller, *Helen Keller's Journal: 1936–1937*, Doubleday, Doran & Co., 1938, p. 60.
44. Mary Wollstonecraft, English writer, philosopher and women's rights advocate; from *A Vindication of the Rights of Woman*, 1792, W.W. Norton & Co., 1975, chapter 4, pp. 54–55.
45. Washington Irving, American author, historian and diplomat; from his story "The Wife" written in 1819, in *The Sketch Book of Geoffrey Crayon, Gent.*, Oxford University Press, 2009, p. 29.
46. The Apostle Paul, Roman citizen, Jew, Pharisee, persecutor of Christians, convert to Christianity and Apostle who spread the news about Jesus throughout the Mediterranean; from his letter to the church at Philippi around 60 AD, *Philippians* 4:12 (NIV translation of the Bible).
47. Brené Brown, *Daring Greatly*, p. 137.

48. King Solomon, *Book of Proverbs* 19:8 (NKJV translation of the Bible).
49. Helen Bevington, American poet, diarist, essayist and English literature professor; from *When Found, Make a Verse Of,* Simon & Schuster, 1961, p. 34.
50. C.S. Lewis, *Selected Literary Essays,* Cambridge University Press, 1969, p. 99.
51. King David, defeater of Goliath, King of Judah and later the second King of the United Kingdom of Israel and Judah (c. 1010–970 BC); from the *Book of Psalms* 19:8 (TV translation of the Bible).
52. See the 1st-century letter written by James, brother of Jesus, son of Joseph and Mary, Jew and leader of the early Christian church; *James* 1:5.
53. Elle Macpherson (born 1964), Australian model, TV host and actor.
54. Reinhold Niebuhr (1892–1971), American theologian, ethicist, political and social commentator, and seminary professor; originally drafted in the 1930s with this version finalised by 1951.
55. King Solomon, *Book of Proverbs* 23:4 (NIV translation of the Bible).
56. John Donne, English poet, priest, lawyer and parliamentarian; from Josiah H. Gilbert, *Dictionary of Burning Words of Brilliant Writers*, Wilbur B. Ketcham, 1895, p. 191.
57. Jesus, from the account of Jesus' life written by his disciple Matthew, *Matthew* 11:28–29 (NIV translation of the Bible).
58. Martha Graham, American modern dance legend and choreographer; from Agnes de Mille, *Martha: The Life and Work of Martha Graham*, Random House, 1991, p. 264.
59. Diane Paddison, *Work Love Pray*, Zondervan, 2011, p. 221.
60. King Solomon, *Book of Proverbs* 3:7–8 (LB translation of the Bible) .
61. Martin Luther King Jr, American Baptist minister, humanitarian, leader and activist in the African-American civil rights movement; from his 1967 Massey Lectures, reproduced in *The Trumpet of Conscience*, Beacon Press, 1968, p. 79.
62. Alice Walker, *Overcoming Speechlessness: A Poet Encounters the Horror in Rwanda, Eastern Congo, and Palestine/Israel*, Seven Stories Press, 2010, pp. 59–60.
63. Francis Schaeffer, American theologian, philosopher, writer and pastor; from *The God Who Is There*, Hodder & Stoughton, 1968, p. 146.
64. Mother Teresa, born to Albanian parents, Roman Catholic nun, missionary to Calcutta, India, and recipient of the Nobel Peace Prize; from *Mother Teresa: A Simple Path*, compiled by Lucinda Vardey, Ballantine Books, 1995, p. 79.
65. King David, *Book of Psalms* 23:1–3 (ESV translation of the Bible).
66. The Apostle Paul, from his letter to the church at Rome, *Romans* 8:6 (NKJV translation of the Bible).

67. Written a seriously long time ago BC; from the first book of the Bible, *Genesis* 1:1 (NIV translation of the Bible).

68. Madeleine L'Engle, American writer, novelist and Newbery Medal winner; from *Walking on Water: Reflections on Faith and Art*, WaterBrook Press, 1998, p. 101.

69. Julia Cameron, American author, artist and teacher; from *The Artist's Way: A Course in Discovering and Recovering Your Creative Self*, Pan Books, 1995, p. 181.

70. Edward de Bono, Maltese writer, intellectual champion of lateral thinking, educational psychologist and consultant; from *Serious Creativity: Using the Power of Lateral Thinking to Create New Ideas,* HarperBusiness, 1992, p. 73.

71. Attributed to Cheryl Hughes.

72. Spoken by Atticus Finch to his daughter Scout, in a novel by an American novelist who received the Pulitzer Prize for Fiction; Harper Lee, *To Kill a Mockingbird*, Grand Central Publishing, 1960, chapter 11, pp. 139–140.

73. King Solomon, *Book of Proverbs* 16:17 (NKJV translation of the Bible).

74. Attributed to C.S. Lewis (1898–1963); and to many others over the years.

75. Written by someone who had read Reinhold Niebuhr's *Serenity Prayer*.

76. An ancient Jewish teacher, *Book of Ecclesiastes* 3:1, 4 (NIV translation of the Bible).

77. King Solomon, *Book of Proverbs* 17:22 (RSV translation of the Bible).

78. Marjorie Pay Hinkley (1911–2004), American mother of five children, wife of the President of the Church of Jesus Christ of Latter-Day Saints in Salt Lake City; from Gordon Hinckley, *Small and Simple Things*, Deseret Books, 2003, p. 126.

79. William Shakespeare, English playwright, actor and poet; from his *Sonnet 116*, 1609.

80. Mother Teresa, *A Simple Path*, p. 79.

81. Mahatma Gandhi (1869–1948), Indian lawyer, non-violent civil rights activist, leader of the Indian independence movement; as quoted in O.P. Dhiman, *Betrayal of Gandhi*, Kalpaz Publications, 2010, p. 86. For the same words, see also Spurgeon's 1882 sermon in Charles H. Spurgeon, *Spurgeon's Sermons on Prayer*, Hendrickson Publishers, 2007, p. 477.

82. The Apostle John, fisherman, one of the disciples of Jesus; from his first letter in the Bible, *1 John* 4:7–8 (NIV translation of the Bible).

83. The Apostle Paul, from his letter to the church in Ephesus, *Ephesians* 4:26 (ESV translation of the Bible).

84. A Psalmist (possibly King David), from the *Book of Psalms* 94:19 (NKJV translation of the Bible).

85. Brené Brown, *The Gifts of Imperfection: Your Guide to a Wholehearted Life*, Hazelden, 2010, pp. 57–58.

86. Anne Manne, *The Life of I,* p. 239.
87. See the first letter to Timothy written by the Apostle Paul, *1 Timothy* 6:10 (NIV translation of the Bible).
88. Timothy Keller with Katherine Leary Alsdorf, *Every Good Endeavour: Connecting Your Work to God's Plan for the World*, Hodder & Stoughton, 2012, p. 37.
89. Betty Friedan, "Feminism Takes a New Turn", *New York Times Magazine*, 18 November, 1979, p. 98.
90. Valerie Volk, educator and writer from Adelaide, South Australia, www.valerievolk.com.au.
91. See the first book of the Bible, *Genesis* 3:17–19.
92. Annabel Crabb, *The Wife Drought*, Random House, 2014, p. 37.
93. Annabel Crabb, p. 254.
94. She is depicted as a wool classer, fibre assessor, textile worker, knitter and weaver; a food importer; a small business owner and manager; a land valuer and property developer; an entrepreneur, agriculturalist and viticulturist; an investor and commercial trader; a caretaker and maintenance worker; a textile industry spinner and thread maker; an interior designer; a fashion designer and tailor; a draper, retailer and salesperson; and a manufacturer and wholesaler of accessories. See the *Book of Proverbs* 31:10–31.
95. *Genesis* 1:26–29.
96. Jesus, from the account of Jesus' life written by his disciple Matthew, *Matthew* 6:21 (NIV translation of the Bible).
97. Peter Fitzsimons, *Nancy Wake: A Biography of Our Greatest War Heroine*, HarperCollins, 2002, pp. 354–358.
98. *American Time Use Survey*, Bureau of Labor Statistics, United States Department of Labor, 2013, http://www.bls.gov/tus/charts/#about.
99. *How Australians Use Their Time*, Australian Bureau of Statistics, 2006, www.abs.gov.au.

Abbreviations

Common English Bible (CEB); Darby Translation (DBY); Douay-Rhiems 1899 American Edition (DRA); English Standard Version (ESV); God's Word Translation (GWT); King James Version (KJV); The Living Bible (LB); Lexham English Bible (LEB); The Message (MSG); New American Standard Bible (NAS); New International Reader's Version (NIRV); New International Version (NIV); New King James Version (NKJV); New Living Translation (NLT); New Revised Standard Version (NRSV); Revised Standard Version (RSV); The Voice (TV); World English Bible (WEB); Wycliffe Bible (WYC).

Photographs

All colour pictures are stock photography from istockphoto.com. The best efforts to source the black and white photos are:

- *Chapter 2, Generosity*: American women serving unemployed men soup and bread in Los Angeles, California, January 1930 (Hulton Archive, Getty Images).
- *Chapter 3, Sociability*: Victorian women at afternoon tea, circa 1901 (US Library of Congress).
- *Chapter 4, Unity*: Miss Margaret McKay and her students near Milton, North Dakota, 1913 (Fred Hultstrand History in Pictures Collection, NDIRS-NDSU, Fargo).
- *Chapter 5, Intimacy*: Nineteenth-century Chinese women styling hair.
- *Chapter 6, Beauty*: A female Victorian traveller at the Pilgrim's Rest in Burma, circa 1900.
- *Chapter 7, Equity*: An English suffragette being arrested, circa 1913.
- *Chapter 8, Opportunity*: Mary Arnold, an Aviation Machinist's Mate in the US Navy Reserve, working on an SNJ training plane at the Naval Air Station in Jacksonville, Florida, 4 November 1943 (US National Archives and Records Administration).
- *Chapter 9, Adversity*: A female mountaineer climbing a rock face in the 1930s (Getty Images).
- *Chapter 10, Clarity*: Lydia Maria Child (1802–1880), American writer, abolitionist and women's rights advocate, reading a book in 1870 (US Library of Congress).
- *Chapter 11, Serenity*: Jewish women praying on Jewish New Year along the Williamsburg Bridge in New York City, 1909.
- *Chapter 12, Vitality*: Three women riding bicycles with modern pneumatic tires in 1884 (George D. McDowell Philadelphia Evening Bulletin Photograph collection).
- *Chapter 13, Spirituality*: Two children praying with their mother, from a picture in a book with the caption "Now I Lay Me Down to Sleep", circa late 1800s.
- *Chapter 14, Creativity*: Marianne North (1830–1890), English traveller, naturalist and botanical artist, painting in the outdoors, circa 1880.
- *Chapter 15, Integrity*: American Judge Florence E. Allen (1884–1966) seated in her chambers, circa 1920-1929; the first woman to be elected to a US state Supreme Court when she was elected to the Ohio Supreme Court in 1920 (Columbus Dispatch P 245).
- *Chapter 16, Levity*: Flappers dancing across a building in Paris, circa 1920s.
- *Chapter 17, Love*: A young couple with their baby, circa 1912.

Index

About the Author

Anne Winckel is a farmer's daughter from South Australia who studied law, arts and education at the University of Adelaide. After working in both high schools and universities, Anne moved to Melbourne to complete her Master's in constitutional law and to lecture at the University of Melbourne.

Anne assumed she would remain in the education sector when she accidentally got a job as a legal recruitment consultant. After nine years in recruitment, she launched her own legal and executive search firm in Melbourne – Delta Partners. Anne has previously been on the board of Australian Women Lawyers, and she is currently a member of Victorian Women Lawyers (where she was on the executive committee for many years), the Australian Corporate Lawyers Association and the Law Institute of Victoria.

Anne's two main vocations – education and recruitment – have given her 25 years of observing the way professional women make career plans and then sometimes ignore, or merely survive those plans. She has been the inaugural convenor of two groups for business and professional women: *Beyond the Glass Ceiling* in Adelaide and the *Soul Food Breakfast Club* in Melbourne – groups aimed at encouraging women personally, spiritually and professionally.

Anne is a speaker and presenter on topics such as "Navigating Your Accidental Career", "Is Your Soul Going Down the Corporate Black Hole?" and "Survival Tips for the Time-Poor Pandemic."

Anne is also a participant in the training program being run by a beautiful little white dog called Billy.

Contacting the Author

Visit Anne's website, **www.annewinckel.com** to contact the author, find out about her next book and investigate her seminars and presentations.

www.ingramcontent.com/pod-product-compliance
Lightning Source LLC
Chambersburg PA
CBHW021036210326
41598CB00016B/1043